# TEDDY
# BEARS

# TEDDY BEARS

### THE COLLECTOR'S GUIDE TO SELECTING, RESTORING AND ENJOYING NEW AND VINTAGE TEDDY BEARS

**Margaret and Gerry Grey**

THE
APPLE
PRESS

A QUINTET BOOK

Published by The Apple Press
6 Blundell Street
London N7 9BH

ISBN 1–85076–522–7

This book was designed and produced by
Quintet Publishing Limited
6 Blundell Street
London N7 9BH

Creative Director: Richard Dewing
Designer: Ian Hunt
Project Editor: Katie Preston
Editor: Alison Leach
Photographers: Nick Bailey and Jeremy Thomas

Typeset in Great Britain by
Central Southern Typesetters, Eastbourne
Manufactured in Singapore by
Bright Arts Pte Limited
Printed in China by
Leefung-Asco Printers Limited

## AUTHORS' DEDICATION

To mum, dad and family and all of our teddy bear
friends the world over. Particular thanks and
appreciation to those people past, present and future
who ever wanted to write about or make a teddy bear
– without their pioneering spirit there would be no
need for this book. And especially to grandson Karl,
who seems to have inherited our love and enthusiasm
for teddy bears.

# CONTENTS

**INTRODUCTION** *6*

**1 FROM TOY BEAR TO TEDDY BEAR (1903–18)** *9*

**2 BETWEEN THE WARS (1919–39)** *19*

**3 POST-WAR RECOVERY (1946–60)** *30*

**4 THE AGE OF SPECIAL EDITION BEARS** *40*

**5 THE ERA OF THE TEDDY BEAR ARTIST** *54*

**6 WHERE AND HOW TO BUY** *66*

**7 CARE AND REPAIRS** *73*

**8 LEARNING MORE ABOUT BEARS** *77*

**INDEX** *79*

**ACKNOWLEDGMENTS** *80*

# INTRODUCTION

It is only about 15 years since a talented but obscure actor, Peter Bull, whose face was instantly recognizable but whose name is hardly ever remembered, first alerted people to the joys of collecting teddy bears by talking with such enthusiasm about them on British and American television. At the time it was unusual to know precisely what an arctophile is – a person who loves teddy bears – let alone be a collector of teddy bears.

The USA, which was and still is the world's leading teddy bear nation, provided the necessary driving force for this new phenomenon to continue into the 1980s, but several years passed before it spread to other parts of the world. Teddy bear collecting is now, however, one of the most popular collecting interests worldwide. Prices for all bears have escalated in recent years, culminating in the record-breaking sale at auction (for £55,000/$86,000) of "Happy" in 1989. All collectors naturally live in hope that one day they will find their own "Happy", but teddy bear collecting is so much more than good investment.

Over the years, many authors have tried to analyse precisely what the appeal of a teddy bear is. Although

LEFT **The bear on the left is a Gebrüder Bing from 1911 and the one on the right is a Chiltern Hugmee c. 1930.**

ABOVE **"Happy" – a 1926 Steiff – is seen here in her role as mascot of the authors' "Teddies of the World '93" convention.**

challenging, we think this is quite unnecessary and probably an impossible task. In our opinion though, "Happy" seems to epitomize the sheer beauty and character we all seek in our teddy bears – gaze into those great big eyes and your heart just melts! It is precisely this reaction that should be experienced with any bear – love and appreciation – rather than thinking about its potential as an investment. Collect only what appeals to you and not just what you think might be valuable and that way you will not be disappointed. In fact for the majority of people the most "precious" bear, regardless of financial investment, in their collection will be the first bear they ever owned, loved and cherished since childhood.

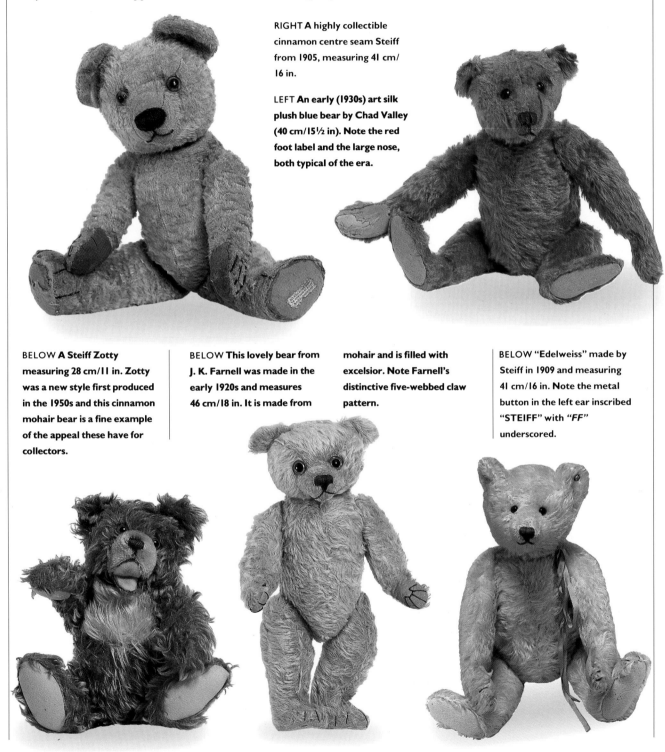

RIGHT **A highly collectible cinnamon centre seam Steiff from 1905, measuring 41 cm/ 16 in.**

LEFT **An early (1930s) art silk plush blue bear by Chad Valley (40 cm/15½ in). Note the red foot label and the large nose, both typical of the era.**

BELOW **A Steiff Zotty measuring 28 cm/11 in. Zotty was a new style first produced in the 1950s and this cinnamon mohair bear is a fine example of the appeal these have for collectors.**

BELOW **This lovely bear from J. K. Farnell was made in the early 1920s and measures 46 cm/18 in. It is made from** mohair and is filled with excelsior. Note Farnell's distinctive five-webbed claw pattern.

BELOW **"Edelweiss" made by Steiff in 1909 and measuring 41 cm/16 in. Note the metal button in the left ear inscribed "STEIFF" with *"FF"* underscored.**

This book is intended to provide you with examples of some of the bears you might wish to add to your collection and tell you more about those you already have. It is not about what we own or want to collect – although some of our preferences are naturally given – but more a cross-section of collectible bears to help guide you. In a book of this size it is impossible to do justice to the whole spectrum of bears and we have concentrated in general on bears that are available and therefore affordable although a few rare examples have been included. So, whether your preference is for "old" bears (pre 1960), contemporary manufactured bears or artist-designed teddy bears, good bear-hunting and good luck!

LEFT **A one-off artist bear by Barbara Conley c. 1993, measuring 56 cm/22 in. Using traditional materials, Barbara has managed to recapture the character of the early bears.**

RIGHT **These one-off bears were produced for the authors in 1991. They are the result of a collaboration between two of the world's top artists – Joan Woessner and Steve Schutt.**

## THE ORIGINAL TEDDY BEAR MAN

In the late 1970s Peter Bull (PB) brought about a great change in the teddy bear world. Because he readily talked about his passion for bears, people felt they too could openly admit to caring for and amassing hordes of old and new teddy bears. Contrary to popular belief PB was not a collector but his doors were ever open to "waifs and strays". His favourites were probably "Theodore", "Delicatessen" and "Bully" bear. Following Theodore's appearance on *The Tonight Show* in the USA, a Miss Euphemia Ladd of Sacco, Maine, asked if her old bear could come and live with "Theodore". The bear was christened "Delicatessen" and was later to star as "Aloysius" in the television programme *Brideshead Revisited*. On May 21 1984, Peter Bull, DSC, died of a heart attack aged 72. He is sadly missed but he would be delighted if he could see the fun and joy that resulted from his efforts.

# FROM TOY BEAR TO TEDDY BEAR (1903–18)

CHAPTER

The true origins of the teddy bear probably go back to the Middle Ages when so-called civilized people were fascinated by real wild bears. Unfortunately, these poor tortured and abused beasts were used throughout Europe purely for entertainment – as dancing bears. Hundreds of years later the Victorians began the trend for real bears to be kept in zoos – again for the entertainment and education of the masses.

At the end of the 19th century Stuttgart Zoo in Germany was frequently visited by a young toy designer from Giengen-en-Brenz named Richard Steiff, a nephew of the renowned toy producer Margarete Steiff. He was interested in all animals but bears particularly intrigued him. Life-like bears had been made by Steiff for some five or six years previously but they were based on fully grown bears, and were therefore difficult to play with. Richard sketched little bear cubs and it was these that influenced Steiff's prototype of the first toy bear late in 1902.

This toy bear was part of a small range of movable (*Beweglich*) animals employing disc joints (*angeschiebt*) which formed part of a shipment of toys to New York around the middle of February 1903. Its general shape and appearance closely resembled a real bear with a long shaven snout, very long arms, stout body, big feet and the quite distinctive back hump.

It is important to consider the period of time required for designing and then producing this new range. Clifford Berryman's famous cartoon of President Theodore (Teddy) Roosevelt appeared in the *Washington Post* on November 16, 1902. Communications in those days were so limited that we doubt that this cartoon could have had any influence on Richard Steiff, as is often suggested.

However, it is thought, though not substantiated, that the cartoon was responsible for Russian immigrants Morris and Rose Michtom, who were novelty and stationery storekeepers of Brooklyn, New York, creating the first toy bears made in America.

LEFT **The 1908 cover of *The Sketch* picturing a teddy bear at the Chicago rally to elect President Taft. The caption is "Teddy Bear in Politics: the Cause of the Rumpus".**

Subsequently – and presumably rather later in 1903 – the Michtoms' toy bears were bought by a large wholesale company, Butler Bros., and distributed throughout the USA.

We believe it would take a considerable time to design, develop and then make a range of quality prototype toys for export to the USA. Commonsense therefore suggests that Steiff's own toy bear was in fact the world's first! However, both Steiff and the Michtoms, who set up The Ideal Novelty and Toy Co., can justly claim they were pioneers of the original teddy bear. The dramatic last-minute purchase of 3,000 of Steiff's bears at the Leipzig Toy Fair in March 1903 by Herman Berg of Geo Borgfeldt, the world-famous American toy importers, when everyone else had ignored them, was incredibly fortuitous.

While Steiff's bear closely resembles a real bear, the Ideal version is much more similar to Berryman's own cartoon bear cub and, therefore, rather more like the teddy bear we know. Clifford Berryman continued to draw many cartoons associated with President Roosevelt, and, eventually, these were probably the greatest single influence in coining the term "teddy bear" that we now so affectionately use.

During those early years both firms developed their ranges, but it was not very long before Steiff's greater experience of toy design and production, coupled with Richard's imaginative ideas for bears of such variety and sheer quality, enabled them to become the world's premier manufacturer. Conversely, Ideal's bears appear to have hardly changed from their first design.

Steiff's first bear in 1903 was referred to as the 55PB, followed by the 35PB in early 1904. Both used disc joints held together by a strong string cord. Unfortunately, these were found to be rather impractical, and broke so easily that Steiff changed briefly to using double wires, but this proved to be far too dangerous. This led quickly to the development of the famous rod bears where a metal rod was passed through the upper body of the bear attaching the arms, with a vertical T-rod connecting and supporting the head, and another rod attaching the legs. The head was stuffed from the top and to facilitate this, a horizontal seam from ear to ear was provided. This bear is usually referred to as the 28PB.

Unfortunately, this bear was rather awkward in its movement and its large rotund body really did not have sufficient child appeal. After only a year (1905), this led to the production of the *Barle* (meaning someone dear) range of PAB bears. Their great virtue was that they were softer, filled with a mixture of excelsior and kapok, thus making them far more cuddly than their

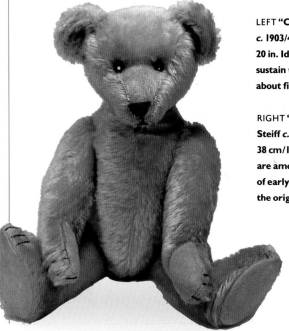

LEFT **"Charlamagne" by Ideal,** *c.* 1903/4 and measuring 51 cm/ 20 in. Ideal were only able to sustain this quality and style for about five years.

RIGHT **"Christian Gabriel" by Steiff** *c.* 1903/4, measuring 38 cm/15 in. These rod bears are among the most desirable of early Steiffs, especially with the original wax nose.

predecessors, and significantly more appealing to children!

This was a great breakthrough and the turning point for Steiff who had experienced great difficulty during the first few years with acceptance of their toy bears. The PAB35 is assumed to have been the first of a range that came in seven sizes from 17 cm/6½ in up to 80 cm/ 32 in, but because the bear was lighter in weight and the articulated body was held together by a conventional double disc joint and metal pin, it had a more acceptable and reliable movement. (Incidentally, to establish the size of this range of bears always measure in the *seated* position to the top of its head.)

Around the same time Richard Steiff also produced his now famous prototype – a small grey bear referred to as model 5322 (5 = movable, 3 = mohair and 22 = size (33 cm/13 in)). Steiff's archives suggest that only two of these were made and perhaps a few others as samples. Quite definitely this must be one of the rarest and possibly the most valuable bear on earth. An example can be found in the Steiff Museum.

Franz Steiff, another of Margarete's nephews, had the previous year decided to implement a trademark standard by introducing the metal button in the ear "Knopf im Ohr", a symbol used ever since. Initially, the elephant button was used, followed later that year

LEFT **The nickel-plated Steiff elephant button is supposed to have been the first unregistered trademark "Knopf im Ohr". It was followed by a blank button and then in 1905 by a button embossed with "STEIFF".**

(1904) by a plain blank button (not to be confused with the blank blue button used briefly between 1948 and 1950), superseded in May 1905 by an inscribed STEIFF button when Steiff finally had their unique trademark confirmed.

There is some controversy over the exact dating of the buttons – most authorities now suggest the order we give but others believe the blank button came first. Both may have been used simultaneously, although we suspect the elephant button was possibly the first because this happened to be Steiff's logo at the time. Logic, however, suggests the blank button might have been used initially simply because it was easier and more convenient to produce. In the USA in 1906, the name "Teddy" was adopted and the ubiquitous "teddy bear" was officially christened.

Meanwhile, in the USA teddy bear manufacturers were emerging (mainly around New York), who

LEFT **This PAB 43 (right) from 1905 is shown here with a modern replica of a PAB 35. The original bear marked a successful change of direction for Steiff.**

RIGHT **"Still Hope" by Aetna from _c._ 1907/08. This company were probably the best American bear maker in the early days as can be seen from this lovely example.**

probably drew on the experience and knowledge of emigrant toy workers flocking there from Europe. Despite innumerable claims by American manufacturers that their bears compared in quality to those from Steiff, they emphatically did not! One thing, however, we have to thank those early American firms for was their inventiveness – bears that whistled, musical bears, and of course the redoubtable bright-eyed teddy, which had eyes illuminated by an inbuilt battery – were but a few of the intriguing new features they gave to teddy bears. It was this flair for the unusual that influenced manufacturers in other countries.

Teddy bear manufacture did not begin in the UK until 1908 when J. K. Farnell began production. Unfortunately the British public were not immediately enthralled by their bears and Farnells were forced to export almost their entire stock to the USA, South Africa and even Germany! Evidence of other British manufacturers from this period is very sketchy and unreliable and positive identification will be difficult.

The world trade in teddy bears reached its peak in 1907 when Steiff's production alone was a little under 1,000,000 teddy bears. Some companies that sprang up simply produced imitations of Steiff bears but there were innovators such as Gebrüder Bing. They were responsible for developing the clockwork mechanism for bears (1908–10) used for roller-skating bears, acro or tumbling bears and even bears pushing balls. The boom was followed almost immediately by a slump during which several manufacturers in Germany and the USA ceased trading overnight. Some new companies did appear such as Schuco (Schreyer and Co) and Gebrüder Hermann Kg. With the outbreak of war in 1914, German goods were prohibited in the UK and the instant demise of the competition persuaded several British companies to start teddy bear production. Many companies began by copying Steiff products, but it was not long before the skills developed sufficiently to start producing original designs for good quality bears.

LEFT **"Sergeant Culver"**, *c.* **1907/08, measures 51.5 cm/ 20¼ in. The manufacturer of this splendid bear is unknown.**

BELOW **A splendid cinnamon Steiff measuring 40 cm/15¾ in.**

**It was made at the height of Steiff's early success** *c.* **1907/08.**

RIGHT **This bright eyes bear was made by the Stuffed Toy Co** *c.* **1917 and measures 43 cm/ 17 in.**

# COLLECTOR'S NOTEBOOK 1903-18

These early formative years provide the serious collector with their greatest challenge and, needless to say, expense. Fortunately many top quality teddy bears have survived and what wonderful and lovable characters they can be. (Note: the dates indicate the first known year of production.)

## USA

### AETNA TOY ANIMAL CO (1906)

▌ Look for the printed oval trademark "AETNA", usually stamped across the centre of the bear's left foot pad, quite often indistinct but traces can usually be found if you look carefully.

▌ These bears are wonderful with such lovely appealing faces, and, in our view, probably represent the best of all American bears from this period.

▌ Rare and extremely hard to find because the firm only existed for around two years are very collectible.

BELOW **A bear from the Bruin Manufacturing Co c. 1907/08, measuring 32 cm/12½ in. Many American companies failed after only a few years and this makes their bears even more desirable and sought after.**

### BRUIN MANUFACTURING CO (1907)

Look for the woven black label with B.M.C. inscribed in gold letters and fixed centrally across the breadth of the right foot.

The bears have wide-apart ears with rather triangular shaped heads.

▌ These bears are highly collectible though scarce because this firm only existed from about 1907 to 1909.

### HARMAN MANUFACTURING CO (1907)

▌ Appearance rather similar to Ideal bears which could create identification difficulties. Something unusual they did make to look for is a "Teddy Shopper" (handbag size) in white or cinnamon mohair which came in three sizes (25 cm/10 in, 30 cm/12 in and 40 cm/14 in).

### HECLA BEAR CO (1907)

▌ These attractive bears will be particularly difficult to identify due to their close resemblance to Steiff bears of the same period. They appear, however, to stand rather differently and the wide placing of the ears appears more typical of American bears than Steiff.

▌ Rust-coloured yarn was normally used for forming noses and mouths.

### IDEAL TOY AND NOVELTY CO (1903)

The first of the American bear manufacturers. Early examples are very elusive and difficult to authenticate. The appearance of Ideal bears is, however, quite distinctive and they are very appealing and collectible.

▌ Unfortunately, the company seems to have adopted similar designs for quite a long time and to some extent this detracts from their collectibility.

▌ It should be possible to find bears from this era in good condition and not too expensive compared with German bears of the same genre.

▌ Look out particularly for the small 15 cm/6 in googly-eyed bear made around 1904 based on the Clifford Berryman cartoon (supposed to have been given away during Theodore Roosevelt's election campaign). A larger 30 cm/12 in size continued to be made until *circa* 1912 and is not so valuable.

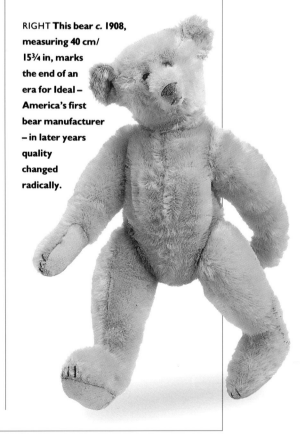

RIGHT **This bear c. 1908, measuring 40 cm/15¾ in, marks the end of an era for Ideal – America's first bear manufacturer – in later years quality changed radically.**

**OTHER AMERICAN MANUFACTURERS**

**THE AMERICAN DOLL & TOY MANUFACTURING CO (1907)** Produced electric bright-eyed teddies and the celebrated "White House" teddy bear with a voice, ribbon and bell, rather similar to Steiff except for flat-bottomed feet. Claimed their bears were the only American made bears to be equal to the imported bears (Steiff). Sole agents were Baker and Gigler Company.

**COLUMBIA TEDDY BEAR MANUFACTURING (1907)** Were responsible for the "Laughing Roosevelt" bears which are still to be found albeit with difficulty.

**DREAMLAND DOLL COMPANY (1907)** Produced a topsy turvy half teddy–half doll separated by skirt. Rare and hard to find.

**B. EPSTEIN (1907)** Little known except they advertised their bears in 1907 (*Playthings*).

**FAST BLACK SHIRT CO (1907)** Produced teddy bears with electric bright eyes.

**MRS G.C. GILLISPIE (1907)** Produced and patented a tumbling teddy bear.

**GUND MANUFACTURING CO (1906)** Thought to have produced a small range of teddy bears but these early bears have so far not been definitely identified.

ABOVE **A "Laughing Roosevelt" bear from Columbia Teddy Bear Manufacturers c. 1907 measuring 43 cm/ 17 in. The mouth can be operated by squeezing the stomach.**

**HAHN AND AMBERG (1907)** Advertised their teddy bear dolls.

**MILLAR MANUFACTURING CO (1906)** Advertised in 1907 the "'Antiseptic Bear' for the most cleanliness" which came in cinnamon, white and other unspecified colours.

**ROUECH-BOWDEN (1907)** A company from Chicago and another who appears to have based its designs on Steiff.

**STRAUSS MANUFACTURING CO (1907)** Produced wonderful musical and self-whistling teddy bears.

**UNCLE REMUS STUFFED TOYS (1907)** Distributed by A.S. Ferguson & Company, Uncle Remus produced bears with a special patented eye-fixing method which ensured "permanent uniformity" in positioning the eyes and retaining the head shape. Could have been based on Charles Sackmans invention patent 844,619 in November 1908.

**WHITESON COMPANY (1907)** Advertised "Prices The Lowest: Largest Sizes and Workmanship the Best", but nothing else is known.

---

## TEDDY DISTRIBUTORS IN THE USA

Influential importers/wholesalers who distributed teddy bears throughout the USA at that time are worth mentioning. Many of them persuaded manufacturers to make and supply bears, some of which they may have marketed under their own names.

**GEO BORGFELDT & COMPANY** was the greatest of all these firms and was responsible for that first eventful purchase of 3,000 teddy bears from Steiff at the Leipzig Spring Toy Fair in 1903. Had they not done this, we might never have had a teddy bear craze at all! Borgfeldt's influence on the toy industry was legendary.

**BUTLER BROS.** subsequently took over the marketing and distribution of the early Ideal Toy and Novelty Co teddy bears. They also distributed a range of Steiff bears from about 1908 onwards.

**STROBEL & WILKEN CO** were notable as distributors for BMC.

**E.L. HORSMAN & COMPANY** were distributors for Hecla and Aetna bears (*see* page 13). It was Horsman & Co who first used the name "teddy" in an advertisement in the American trade magazine *Playthings* in December 1906.

## U K

### ATLAS MANUFACTURING CO (1914)

This was another firm who had changed from making sports goods to teddy bears.

▌ In 1916 *The Toy and Fancy Goods Trader* reported the Atlas range as 30 varieties of teddies from 22 cm/8½ in to 2.15 m/7 ft high; coloured gold, white or light brown, and with squeakers, chimes and rattles.

▌ As with so many of the early British firms, very little evidence exists to support identification but, so far as we can tell, the bodies of the bears were slightly more German in style but the hands were large and round, with small flattish faces, wide-apart ears and noses which might possibly have had down-turned outer stitching, and inverted Y-shaped mouths stitched tight under their noses.

### BASSETT LOWKE (1910)

This firm was best known for its production of tin-plate toys, particularly railways, but they were reported as having also produced teddy bears.

▌ The great German firm, Gebrüder Bing, which also made locomotives for Bassett Lowke, introduced bears to their range, so it seems probable BL should have done likewise, and it is also conceivable they might have been Bing bears as well. Unfortunately, no records or examples of these bears have so far been found and so we shall probably never be sure.

### CHAD VALLEY CO LTD (1914)

Chad Valley were one of Britain's most successful toy manufacturers.

▌ A retrospective editorial published in *The Toy and Fancy Goods Trader* in August 1922 reported that Chad Valley actually commenced production of their first teddy bear early in 1914 before the outbreak of war.

▌ Frustratingly, no other supportive evidence exists as to the appearance of the bear but we suspect it would probably be similar to the bears they produced in the early 1920s but of course without the early "Chad Valley" or "Aerolite" button which was not registered until 1923.

### DEANS RAG BOOK CO LTD (1915)

Are one of Britain's longest established toymakers.

▌ Although they had made their famous cut-out cloth patterns of teddy bears as early as 1908, apparently it was not until 1915 that Deans decided to make their first proper teddy bear.

▌ No positive details of these bears are currently known.

### J.K. FARNELL (1908)

There is simply insufficient evidence to identify the first bears produced by Farnell positively.

▌ Despite Farnell's excellent reputation, teddies were not at all popular with the domestic market and the company exported most of its production. These early examples are now more likely to be found in the USA than in the UK.

▌ For the moment at least we can only speculate, but a definite pre-1920 Farnell is unknown.

▌ We suspect these teddy bears will probably be somewhat similar to the better known Alpha range of bears produced from the beginning of the 1920s, although as yet we cannot prove this.

### HARWIN & COMPANY (1915)

These bears were very close to Steiff products – not surprising really because their Sales Manager, Mr F. Taylor, represented Steiff for some years!

▌ Harwins are best known for their range of "Ally" bears produced in 1916 – these were bears dressed in various uniforms: British, Scottish, Russian, soldiers, sailors and nurses.

▌ Boy and girl teddies were also produced and in 1917 a teddy bear in pyjamas.

▌ These bears will be quite difficult to find, particularly in good condition and with their original clothes, and will be among the more expensive British bears from this period.

### LEON REES & CO (1915)

In 1915 at their Chiltern Toy Works, L. Rees & Co produced the original Chiltern bear – "Master Teddy".

▌ This rather curious rotund fat-headed little teddy had googly eyes, was dressed in pink and white striped shirt with large bib-type collar, ribbon bow tie and very

BELOW **This is the earliest "Master Teddy" and, as the first Chiltern bear (*c.* 1915, it is rare. It measures 25.5 cm/10 in.**

high-waisted blue trousers with a patch. It has a little red tongue.

▌ It appears to have been available in five sizes and although rare they do exist; good quality ones are expensive.

▌ The first advertisements (1915) indicate the patch was on the left leg and without a chest tag but we have seen bears with the patch on the right leg and with a chest tag indicating "US patent applied for"; these would have been made a year or two later.

### W.J. TERRY (1913)

This firm used the trade name "Terryer Toys".

▌ Their early bears began to establish the stereotype British look, rather than just copying German makers as many others did.

▌ Examples from early advertisements suggest the bears had eyes which glared, large round heads and rather big ears.

▌ Positive identification is difficult.

### OTHER BRITISH MANUFACTURERS

**THOMAS BAXTER (1915)** Produced an illuminated electric eye teddy bear.

### THE BRITISH UNITED TOY MANUFACTURING CO (1914)

Used the trademark "OMEGA" for their soft toy range including bears and "CAMWHEEL" for a soft toy fixed to a metal frame with wooden wheels (similar to the Steiff Record range.

**CRAY AND NICHOLLS (1916)** Reported to have made bears at this time, but no records exist.

**EAST LONDON TOY FACTORY (1915)** Used the trademark "EALON" for their range of soft toys. Examples of these early bears remain unidentified.

### GOTTSCHALK AND DAVIS (1915)

Manufactured bears characterized by ears fixed very high on top of head with a very stern-looking face and arms fixed rather high on shoulders.

### HAWKSLEY & CO (LIVERPOOL) LTD (1916)

Usually produced bears on wheels, similar to Steiff in style and quality.

**IMPERIAL TOY CO (1916)** Reported to have made bears at this time, but no records exist.

**ISAACS (1915)** Used the trade name "ISA" (eventually taken over by Chad Valley Co Ltd).

---

## TEDDY DISTRIBUTORS IN THE UK

During these early formative years there were two major importers and distributors in the UK.

**Josef Eisenmann**, or "Jo" as he was popularly known, was acknowledged as the "King of the Toy Trade" in the UK. Eisenmann & Co were importers and distributors of toys, particularly those from Germany, but it was Jo who suggested to J.K. Farnell that they should make teddy bears to combat the influx of Steiff products. Jo was also the father-in-law of Leon Rees, who eventually in 1920 collaborated with Harry G. Stone to take over the manufacturer of the famous "Chiltern" range.

From 1899 until the outbreak of World War I in 1914, **Herbert E. Hughes** was the sole importer of Steiff products to the UK. In the Ciesliks' book, *Button in the Ear*, they report the close relationship that existed between Otto Steiff and Herbert. Hughes's major clients in Britain were Harrods, Hamleys, Gamages and Josef Eisenmann himself. Because of this association Herbert would almost certainly have had a detailed knowledge of Steiff and the German industry. In 1908 he was responsible for an order of *40,000* Steiff bears just for the UK! Hughes ceased his involvement with Steiff at the outbreak of World War I.

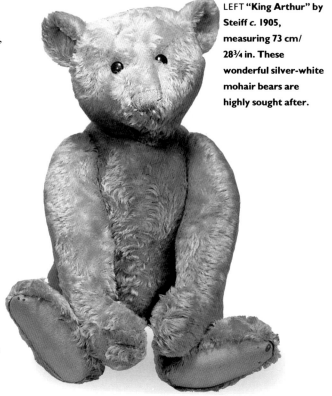

LEFT **"King Arthur" by Steiff** *c.* **1905, measuring 73 cm/ 28¾ in. These wonderful silver-white mohair bears are highly sought after.**

**W.H. Jones (1916)** Some of their bears appear to have had very round bodies and large heads with wide-apart ears, large long arms with upturned wrists but shapeless rod-like legs slightly turned to "stump"-type feet. The noses were unusual, almost batwing-shaped with large down-turned outer stitches.

**Ross Toy Works (1916)** Also used the trade name "HERCULES" so we presume they were associated with the Wholesale Toy Co.

**South Wales Toy Manufacturing Co (1917)** Used the trade name "Madingland". Bears can be distinguished by their large ears fixed close together on top of the head, large nose and long mouth having a rather glum expression. Well-proportioned bodies and arms with distinctive raised circular shaped foot pads with very thick flat insole linings.

**Steevans Musical Toys (1918)** Produced musical chime bears but little else is known at present.

**Teddy Toy Company (1916)** Eventually in the 1920s they adopted the trade name "Softanlite" and claimed the bears would be beautiful and soft, always retaining their shape and their joints never becoming loose. Their early bears have not been identified.

**Wholesale Toy Company (1915)** Used the brand name "Hercules", for their range of soft toys which included teddy bears and a range of wheeled animals.

**Worthing Toy Factory (1915)** Known to have produced teddy bears with the trademark "Humpty Dumpty Toys".

**Wrekin Toy Company (1916)** Eventually taken over by Chad Valley Co Ltd.

**A. Young & Son (1915)** Used the trade name "Jumbo Toys".

## GERMANY

**Gebrüder Bing (1908)**
This firm made highly desirable bears which are surprisingly far scarcer than those produced by Steiff at the time. Expect to have to pay high prices especially for those still in good condition.

▌ The metal arrow-shaped tag fixed in the bear's right ear dates from 1908 to about 1910.

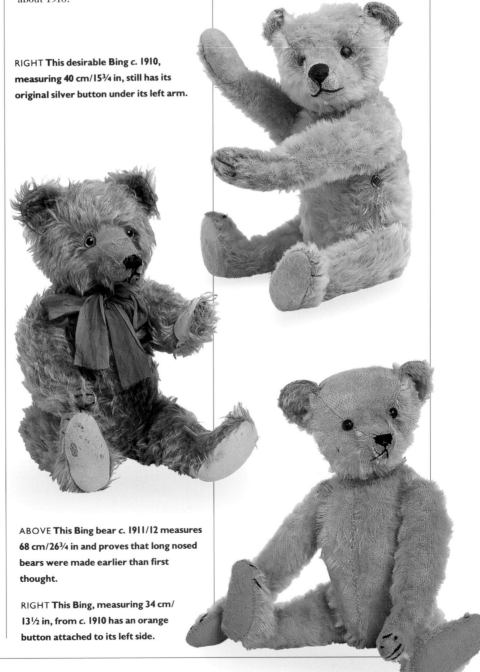

RIGHT **This desirable Bing c. 1910, measuring 40 cm/15¾ in, still has its original silver button under its left arm.**

ABOVE **This Bing bear c. 1911/12 measures 68 cm/26¾ in and proves that long nosed bears were made earlier than first thought.**

RIGHT **This Bing, measuring 34 cm/ 13½ in, from c. 1910 has an orange button attached to its left side.**

▌ A silver metal or orange button fixed to the bear's left side under the arm inscribed with "GBN" suggests the period between 1910 and 1919.

▌ Any early Bing teddy bears, particularly those made from unusual coloured mohair rather than the more conventional light to dark browns, will always be a great attribute to any collection.

### GEBRÜDER HERMANN (1911)

Records of these early bears do not appear to exist and it would therefore be extremely difficult for anyone to identify positively bears from this era.

■ The first labels ever used by Hermann were rosette-style, inscribed BEHA (*BE*rnard *HE*rmann) from about 1911 to 1929. An early Hermann would be a *real* find!

### MARGARETE STEIFF (1903)

Without doubt the world's leading manufacturer, although their bears are highly desirable, they are likely to be extremely difficult to find and expensive. A typical example is the early rod bears from 1904.

■ Should you ever find a 55PB, the first toy bear Steiff made, or a Richard Steiff grey teddy bear, then you could be looking at an absolute fortune.

■ Any of the first PAB soft-filled bears will cost you a substantial amount of money.

■ Black bears (only a small number was made around 1910–12), the hot water bottle bear (only 90 were made between 1907 and 1914), or unusually coloured bears are other valuable finds.

■ Centre seam bears (1904–1906) have wonderful faces and are well regarded, but will also be expensive and scarce.

■ Look for the rarer colours (white and cinnamon) and one with its original button in the left ear but remember these will always attract a premium price.

### OTHER GERMAN MANUFACTURERS

Bears made by any of the following firms will be very difficult to identify. There were many more manufacturers and thriving cottage-industries producing other soft toys and it is almost certain some of these offered teddy bears in their range.

**E. DEHLER (1910–11)** No known details.

**FLEISCHMANN & BLOEDEL (*circa* 1914)** Used the trade name "MICHU".

**CARL HARMUS JR (1909)** Registered a design for a bear with a doll.

**JOHANN HERMANN (1907) (SUCCEEDED BY MAX HERMANN (1920))** Examples of early bears are not known; throughout their time the bears were very similar in appearance to those produced by cousins, Gebrüder Hermann. From 1920 onwards the trademark "MAHESO" was adopted.

**CARL HOFMANN & CO (1910)** Supposed to have produced the first black teddy bear.

**ERICH LEISTNER (1910)** Used the trade name "ERLE".

**H. JOSEF LEVEN & SPRENGER (1910)** No known details from this early period.

**ERNST LIEBERMANN & CO (1910)** Used the trade name "ELI".

**WILHELM STRUNZ (1908)** Copied Steiff products, so therefore be careful. We would anticipate their bears to be of inferior quality and construction.

LEFT **These white Steiffs *c.* 1907/08, measuring 56 cm/ 22 in, are very collectible.**

BELOW **The Steiff PAB 43, *c.* 1905, 70 cm/27½ in, is a very rare soft-filled bear.**

BELOW **A popular centre seam Steiff *c.* 1905/06, measuring 40 cm/15¾ in.**

242.W.    H.R.H. The DUCHESS of YORK    BEAGLES
          'A TEDDY FOR BABY ELIZABETH'    POSTCARDS.

# BETWEEN THE WARS (1919–39)

Immediately following World War I, a period of instability afflicted world markets and many of the firms who had previously been producing teddy bears suddenly found themselves in financial trouble and had to cease trading.

Steiff, by then a well-established and world-leading manufacturer, experienced tremendous difficulty attempting to re-establish the pre-eminence they had enjoyed during the decade leading up to the war, and their struggle was intensified due mainly to a backlash of resentment in Britain and America. Broadly speaking, the German toy industry had no choice but to adopt lower prices during these inflationary times, and many organizations with a vested interest such as The British Toy Federation rather disparagingly referred to "cheap" German toys which the public should avoid!

The Japanese toy industry, in concert with many of their other industries at the time, were then beginning to expand and their cheaper exports were becoming a threat to all. Elsewhere – France and Australia in particular – manufacturers began producing for their domestic markets.

The USA was the world's largest market for toys but their own domestic teddy bear manufacturing base was by now much depleted. Unfortunately, very few of the new American companies of the time managed to make much of a name for themselves, with the possible exception of Knickerbocker, as consumers preferred the imported bears. Even the well-established firms, such as Ideal and Gund, seemed to lack the ability to produce appealing teddy bears.

The UK, on the other hand, had rather successfully managed to retain almost all of its quality soft toy manufacturing base and it was these companies who were subsequently able to prove their potential for producing original ideas. During the next two decades several British companies were to establish themselves as equal to any. The most notable newcomer in the UK was Merrythought, established in 1930.

LEFT **A British postcard from *c.* 1936 showing HRH the Duchess of York, the future Queen Mother, holding a wonderful English bear from the era, probably by J. K. Farnell.**

ABOVE **This _c._ 1923 bear from J. K. Farnell (66 cm/25 in) has replaced pads, but the quality of early Alphas is apparent.**

ABOVE **This _c._ 1923/4 Chad Valley measures 43 cm/17 in and has the old cream-coloured Aerolite trademark button in its ear.**

ABOVE **Despite its new nose, there is no mistaking this Schuco Yes-No mechanism bear _c._ 1930s, measuring 48 cm/19 in.**

ABOVE **A Peter bear by Gebrüder Süssenguth _c._ 1926, measuring 34 cm/13¼ in. The fierce appearance was not popular with children!**

ABOVE **This lovely white Steiff _c._ 1925/6 measures 35 cm/13¾ in. The remains of a red tag are still attached to the button.**

A popular feature of British bears at the time was the new style of soft-filled bears; the Teddy Toy Company produced "Softanlite", followed by W. J. Terry with "Ahsolight". Chad Valley had the "Aerolite" range and many other manufacturers followed. There was also keen competition to present bears as hygienic toys and the Institute of Hygiene mark of approval was highly coveted. In 1929, just before the Great Depression, the Teddy Toy Company introduced the new and cheaper art silk plush instead of mohair, while Chiltern followed shortly afterwards with their "Silky" teddy and Farnell's "Silkalite" range.

In Germany manufacturing had recommenced after World War I but Steiff were finding things difficult. For some years they had persisted with their old designs, until around 1925 when Richard Steiff wrote from the USA that Steiff bears "appear colourless, sober and insipid". These harsh words seemed just the jolt the company needed and the result was a new generation of imaginative and original designs. It was at this time that "Happy" was produced, though it seems that very few bears of this type were made.

The firm Schreyer and Co, better known as Schuco, began this era with a unique bear design – the "Yes-No" series that had a mechanical linkage device concealed within the tail enabling the head to move up or down (nodding or shaking its head).

The depression (1929–32) had severely weakened the foundations of virtually all teddy bear manufacturers and with the threat of another war, it is not surprising that the genre of bears made during the late 1930s lacked the variety of the previous 30 years.

## COLLECTOR'S NOTEBOOK 1919–39

Due to the large number of teddy bear manufacturers all over the world at this time, you have a good chance of finding high-quality teddy bears from this era. However many of the earlier bears, those from the 1920s for example, made by the more famous quality producers will be expensive.

### USA

**COMMONWEALTH TOY AND NOVELTY CO (1934)** 1937 saw the introduction of a rather unusual "Feed me" bear.

▌ Teddy could be fed by pulling a cord at the back of his head so that his mouth would open to swallow food. The food could be retrieved by unzipping the bear. Although not very attractive, these bears are novel and certainly worth looking for.

### GUND INC (1906)

For a major company it is quite surprising to find there are few examples of teddy bears they made during these early years. So far, few quality bears from this era have ever been properly identified, so these might be quite a find.

### KNICKERBOCKER TOY CO INC (1920s)

This firm had been established for around 70 years when in the 1920s it commenced manufacture of teddy bears.

▌ Their bears are recognizable by their very wide heads and short snouts. Some of their early bears had metal noses, and others had conventional noses.

ABOVE **Despite the facial repairs this is a good example of a Knickerbocker Toy Co bear from the mid-1930s (43 cm/17 in).**

▌ Velveteen pads were used on these bears and the firm seemed to like coloured glass eyes, usually green.

▌ Knickerbocker bears had pale yellow cloth labels stitched into the chest seam with a horseshoe logo inscribed "Knickerbocker Toy Co – New York".

▌ By far and away the best of the American bears made during this era, they remain relatively inexpensive.

### UK

**CHAD VALLEY CO LTD (1914)**

Under the banner of Chad Valley were a number of toy factories but the teddy bears were made at their Wellington (Shropshire) factory.

ABOVE **A great Chad Valley bear from the early 1920s, measuring 71 cm/28 in. Its blue button is still attached to his throat.**

❚ Look for the lovely character bears with a very large triangular nose. However, a bear very reminiscent of this was also advertised in 1935 so be very careful about dates.

❚ One way to tell the age is by the buttons Chad Valley used (if fitted). During the early 1920s they had a broad steel rim with a flat recessed celluloid centre; one "Chad Valley" button is coloured blue and the other "Aerolite" is coloured cream. The "Chad Valley" button may be found fixed to the bear's right ear, back or throat. The "Aerolite" button is usually found fixed to the bear's right ear.

❚ So far as we can tell, *circa* 1930 the buttons were changed for two new types – both the rim and celluloid centre are flush but the centre is now raised and slightly convex. One button is cream coloured and the other blue. These buttons are usually found in the right ear or sometimes on the left side.

❚ Magna (1930s) series of bears are really nice – look for the embroidered blue on white label on the sole of the right foot. Notice it refers to Harborne which was Chad Valley's H.Q. although Chad Valley always stated they only ever made teddy bears at Wellington!

❚ Red lettering embroidered on a white label was introduced in the 1930s along with bears with large oval rather bulbous noses. These are great characters to add to your collection.

❚ Chad Valley were constantly taking over other toy companies either to improve their range or get rid of the competition. In the 1920s they took over the Isaacs & Co whose well-known trademark for soft toys (usually on wheels) had been ISA. In 1931 they acquired Peacock & Co who had manufactured printed wooden blocks.

ABOVE **A Chad Valley c. 1930, measuring 40 cm/16 in, showing the distinctive bulbous nose and red label.**

ABOVE **An unusual Chad Valley "Pooh" bear c. 1929 measuring 21 cm/8½ in.**

ABOVE **The standing bear (63 cm/25 in) is from Chad Valley and has the later ear button. The other is by Peacock (68 cm/ 27 in). Both are from the mid 1930s.**

ABOVE **This unusual Chad Valley bear from the 1930s is made of white mohair and measures 56 cm/22 in. Note the stitching on the feet and the long angled style stitching on the paws which are typical of most Chad Valley bears.**

Around the mid 1930s Chad Valley introduced a "Peacock" range of bear which, so far as we can tell, was really a Chad Valley bear with a different label (red on white, style similar to Chad Valley except it carried the wording "Peacocks – British Toys – London".

An alternative probably earlier label with a Peacock emblem is also known to exist. The Peacock bears we have seen are so remarkably similar to Chad Valley that we believe they were made in Chad's factory but marketed under the Peacock banner. These are a real find and rather scarce.

Any Chad Valley bears from this era are worth collecting, provided they are in good condition, and they ought not be too expensive.

In 1938 Chad Valley were awarded the Royal Warrant and a label fixed to the sole of the left foot carries the Royal Coat of Arms and wording "Toymakers to Her Majesty the Queen". In 1953 this was changed (*see* page 32).

### DEANS RAG BOOK CO LTD (1915)

It is surprisingly difficult to find Deans bears from this period, particularly in good condition.

Deans bears tend to have a triangular flat-shaped head with wide-apart, almost vertically located ears and this distinguishes them from other British bears.

Sadly, Deans bears may have been made from inferior quality mohair which might explain why they are nearly always found badly worn.

A straw coloured label with Deans Rag Book Co Ltd printed in black was stitched lengthwise along the sole of the foot. The reason these labels are often missing is because they were only attached at either end.

ABOVE **Note the distinctive triangle-shaped head of this late 1930s Deans bear. It measures 43 cm/17 in.**

ABOVE **The odd proportions of this 1920s, Farnell suggest that the head and body come from different bears (58 cm/23 in).**

ABOVE **A Farnells bear c. 1925 showing the typical webbed claws and cardboard inserts in canvas feet (50 cm/19½ in).**

### J. K. FARNELL (1908)

Look for the early "Alpha" bears produced in the 1920s; the large bears are the best, always made using the top-quality mohair, filled either with excelsior or kapok or a mixture of both.

Look particularly for the bears with the very distinctive webbing on the paws. The Farnell webbing is quite

ABOVE **One of the new style of Farnells bears c. 1935 that appeared after the factory fire in 1934 (41 cm/16 in).**

different from that used by Merrythought and others, and can easily be recognized by the pronounced triangular shape in the centre of the stitching.

Farnells labelled their teddy bears using both their name, country of origin and trade name "ALPHA TOYS".

Dark blue embroidered lettering on creamy base indicate bears from this era.

ABOVE **This 1930s Merrythought – probably from the M range – has a new nose, but it has its wishbone button and foot label.**

## MERRYTHOUGHT LTD (1930)

Some of the early Merrythought bears have similar distinguishing features to bears produced by other firms, particularly Chad Valley. The two companies had their factories only a few miles apart and one of their directors had previously worked for Chad Valley.

▌ Try to add to your collection Merrythought's early "M" range or "Magnet" bear as it was also known.

▌ Merrythought also introduced a webbing pattern applied to the hand paws (this is a much flatter web formation than the earlier Farnell method and only has four "fingers").

▌ Another distinguishing feature was the use of bright orange felt for pads although of course other colours were also used.

▌ Merrythought adopted the use of a button in the ear for a few years. Shaped and formed similar to the one used by Chad Valley but yellow with a wishbone trademark overwritten by "Hygienic – Merrythought – Toys". The button was usually fitted to the left ear but occasionally it can be found on the back of the bear.

▌ Fortunately, right from the start Merrythought adopted a labelling system of black lettering embroidered on a yellow background which was fitted to the sole of either foot. It was used up until outbreak of World War II.

▌ "Bingie" was soon added to the range of bears (1931). This was a seated bear pattern and was so successful that it continued to be made for several years until 1938. Some "Bingies" are dressed and had cloth bodies and limbs to save cost. The trademark label is found attached to the inside of the lower left leg.

LEFT **Two Merrythought "Bingies", a range produced 1931–1938, from the mid 1930s. The bears measure 25 cm/10 in and 33 cm/13 in.**

RIGHT **A Chiltern "Hugmee" *c.* 1930, measuring 60 cm/24 in. The "Hugmee" was one of the finest quality character British bears ever produced and was made for over 50 years from 1923 onwards.**

ABOVE **A Merrythought from the mid 1930s. It is an unusual colour but still has its button and foot label (48 cm/19 in).**

## H. G. STONE & CO LTD (1920)

The Chiltern range of "Hugmee" from the early 1920s and early 1930s are the real finds and the most desirable. Beautiful coloured, fine quality mohair was used, filled with a mixture of excelsior and kapok the bear truly lived up to its name "Hugmee".

▌ "Hugmees" had flat feet with velveteen pads reinforced with card.

▌ Squeakers were fitted but these are usually found inoperable.

ABOVE **A rare Chiltern bear from the late 1920s, measuring 55 cm/22 in. Note the distinctive "Hugmee" face and body.**

▌ Look for the large nose with its upturned, elongated outer stitching.
▌ Swing-type labels were fitted but you will be extremely lucky to find these still in place. They contained a circular trademark which can be helpful to identify the period. The very first bears 1923–6) have "Chiltern" at the top with an outline of rolling hills centrally

located and overprinted with "Toys" and the trademark at the bottom.
▌ Subsequent labels from *circa* 1926, however, are similar but more decorative with two houses in the left foreground but inscribed "trademark" (top), "Chiltern Toys" (centre) and "Made in England" (bottom). These labels were used until well into the 1950s.
▌ Look for the "Cubby" (baby) range of bears introduced in 1930.

## OTHER BRITISH MANUFACTURERS

**EAST LONDON TOY FACTORY LTD (1915)**
Continued with their "EALON" trademark teddy bears.

**INVICTA TOYS** Established in 1935 but very little is known about this firm.

**LINES BROTHERS/INTERNATIONAL MODEL AIRCRAFT CO LTD (1937)**
Produced the first "Pedigree" range of soft toys in 1937. In 1938 "Pedigree" advertised a teddy bear in their range and this appears to be the first occasion they produced bears.

**LOUIS GOLDBERG (1935)** Offered the "cheapest grade of soft toys that have ever been produced in England" – brave words. The result was a fairly nondescript bear which will be hard to identify due to the millions of similar bears made at the time. Look for square shoulders, close-fitting legs, very pointed tapering arms and a chest tag inscribed "Hygienic Toys" with the word "Teddy" centrally located.

**THE SOUTH WALES TOY MANUFACTURING CO (1917)** Used the trade name "Madingland" but there are no known examples. The bears have unusually large, wrap-around ears which are fixed quite close together on top of the head, and unshaven faces with long extended mouths having a rather forlorn

ABOVE **Lines Brothers (Pedigree) bear from c. 1938 (height 52 cm/21 in). This range continued to be produced until the 1950s.**

look. Bodies and arms follow the German style but the feet are in proportion quite small, round and bulbous, unlike the pre World War I version which were very flat!

**TAH TOYS LTD (1919)** Known to have made a range of bears in all sizes and colours and although we have no examples, a 1919 advertisement indicates typically British-style rounded bodies, large heads, and very large floppy ears and enormously large feet. The noses on these bears were triangular with long vertical lines to short horizontal mouths.

**THE TEDDY TOY CO (1916)** Established during World War I; in the early 1920s introduced and patented (No 133625) the "Softanlite" range of the lightest and softest teddy bears which they claimed to be the first! Their bears, which have not been positively identified, were illustrated in an early 1921 advertisement and appear to have large round faces, big ears, round button-style noses with downturned mouths. This company continued in production well into the 1950s.

ABOVE **The "skater" bear was made by Chiltern in the late 1930s (height 33 cm/13 in). The muff and hat are original.**

## GERMANY

### GEBRÜDER BING (1908)

In 1920 Bing were to change their name to Bing-Werke and therefore the "GBN" button mark used previously was replaced by an orange button with the letters "BW" painted in black. The company closed in 1932.

▌ The button by now had been transferred from the body and attached to the outside of the arm.

▌ Many of the bears manufactured during the previous decade were now reproduced with some changes to faces during the 1920s.

▌ Bing went out of business in 1932, and this of course makes their bears even more attractive.

▌ These bears can be found complete even with their button which is an added bonus.

BELOW **A Bing-Werke bear from 1923/4, measuring 58 cm/23 in. These bears, with their long snouts, are very distinctive.**

### SCHUCO (SCHREYER & CO) (1912)

The fashion of the day in the 1920s was for ladies to carry small purse-type handbags. Consequently, essential cosmetics had to be correspondingly small. How novel then that Schuco should produce in 1924 tiny little teddy bears which could contain all the essentials: perfume atomizer, compact, lipstick and even a whisky flask – for the gentlemen of course! These bears were brightly coloured, made from short bristly mohair attached around a metal body – a range known as "Piccolo". They remain a delightful find for any collector, but in very good condition they will not be cheap!

▌ The miniature mechanical clockwork tumbling bears, though lacking in bear character, are also great fun.

▌ The "Bellhop" produced from 1921 is a real character bear and if found with its red tunic, black trousers, pill box hat and leather strap bag all perfectly intact, is a must for any collection.

▌ Without doubt one of the most sought after and treasured of all will be the "Yes-No" range. These bears can often be found in good condition because Schuco used only quality materials. The "Yes-No Clown" is the rarest of them all.

BELOW **A Schuco compact bear from 1927/8 (height 9 cm/3½ in). This was one of the Piccolo range of novelty bears.**

BELOW **A superb example of quality and character can be seen in this large Schuco from c. 1935 (height 51 cm/20 in). Note the three-pawed hands and feet typical of Schuco bears.**

### MARGARETE STEIFF (1903)

At the time of commencement of the red linen ear tag (1925–34) Steiff were producing some really nice, original bears and these are easily distinguishable from the earlier versions because their faces were now much slimmer, although still pointed, the back hump was now far less pronounced and coloured glass eyes were used. Do look out for these bears; often they can be found in very good condition but they can be rather expensive.

▌ Rare to find are the 1926 soft-filled "Teddy Clown" – multi-coloured brown tipped white mohair version made in 11 sizes, along with a plain coloured "Clown" yellow bear. The latter bear was made with two different neck ruffs – one white with a red border and the other white with a blue border which happens to be the rarest.

▌ The "Petsy" range introduced in 1927 was offered in ten sizes and had the distinctive centre-seam patterned head and was available in tipped mohair and

ABOVE **"Remembering Lou" – a Steiff from *c.* 1927/8 (height 43 cm/16½ in). Blue-eye "Petsy" bears are very hard to find. Note the centre seam and tipped mohair.**

BELOW LEFT **This lovely white Steiff from the 1923/4 (height 58 cm/23 in). Steiff's range and style changed significantly after the mid 1920s.**

BELOW RIGHT **This Steiff was made after 1925 (*c.* 1925/6) as can be seen from the remains of the red tag attached to the button. The bear measures 61 cm/24 in.**

plain gold. Of these the beautiful blue-eyed two-tone mohair bears are definitely the most sought after.

▌ The "Teddy Baby" designed and produced in 1930 came in 11 sizes and was made in many different guises, some with open or closed mouths. These are very popular with collectors.

▌ Produced at the same time was the delightfully grinning bear called "Dicky". More usually this was made from gold mohair in eight sizes and the rarer white version made in five sizes. Around 1936 a cheaper version with inset snout and large feet was made for a few years. You will be very lucky to find "Dicky" bears.

▌ The "Circus" bear, produced from 1936 until 1938 which had snap joints and a neck mechanism enabling the bear's limbs and head to be set to pose, remains one of the rarest bears from this whole era.

▌ Steiff also produced a considerable number of small bears which are popular with collectors.

## OTHER GERMAN MANUFACTURERS

**EDUARD CRAMER (1930)** These hard-to-find bears from the early 1930s, were clearly influenced by Steiff's "Teddy Baby" range and have similar features. A musical and walking bear was based on the Steiff's "Clown" range with the same tipped mohair. One of the main features of their bears was the completely shaven snout. The bears had inset eyes, button style noses and partially open mouths, exposing soft pink felt tongues. It is the latter which is unmistakably Cramer's most distinguishing feature although they also made closed-mouth bears.

**GEBRÜDER HERMANN (1911)** A family firm, under the control of Bernhard Hermann, producing bears in their Sonneberg factory. At the time the bears were fitted with a simple swing tag fixed to the upper chest, with the inscription "BEHA" on it "*BE*" taken from *Be*rnhard and "*HA*" from *Ha*rmann. After 1930 "Beha" was displayed in small writing at the top with "Teddy" in large writing across the centre. They are quite distinctive bears should you ever come across one, the main feature being the totally shaven inset snout with a triangular nose and short mouth. Possibly better known for the brown-tipped mohair bear produced in the mid-1920s. These should not be confused with the almost identical-style bear Hermann made 30 years later.

**MAX HERMANN (1920) (LATER HERMANN-SPIELWAREN)** A range of bears called series 112 in ten sizes was produced in the 1920s. They were quite different from their cousin's (Gebr. Hermann) creations, having unusual stand-up, pointed ears (almost cat-shaped) and long, inverted V-shaped mouths giving them rather forlorn expressions. By the

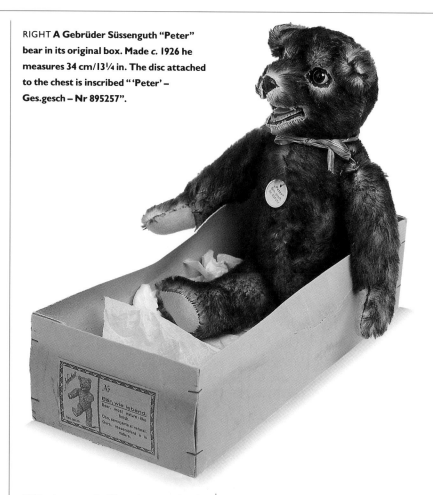

RIGHT **A Gebrüder Süssenguth "Peter" bear in its original box. Made *c.* 1926 he measures 34 cm/13¼ in. The disc attached to the chest is inscribed "'Peter' – Ges.gesch – Nr 895257".**

1930s the range had been increased with series 111 (nine sizes), the main differences being the quality and colour of fabric. These early models carried the trademark "MAHESO". Most bears were exported to the USA.

**H. JOSEF LEVEN & SPRENGER (1910)** Made quite an extensive range of bears. In the 1920s they made eight different styles which expanded to 15 in the 1930s. All appear typically German but otherwise details are limited.

**GEBRÜDER SÜSSENGUTH (1925)** Reputed to have produced several bear designs but the best known was "Peter" bear with its movable eyes, tongue, and open mouth. Made in three sizes and colours, the most common of all is the brown-tipped mohair. It should have a white label with metal rim attached to its

chest. It is still possible to find these bears and recently a small toy factory full of unopened boxed "Peters" was found.

# AUSTRALIA

In general the indigenous teddy bear makers did not commence production until the late 1920s. One striking feature is the close resemblance between Australian bears and those produced by British manufacturers of the day.

**BERLEX TOY PTY**
Another Melbourne-based firm established in the 1930s.

▮ Apparently, the labels were attached to the under side of the left arm.

▮ Berlex bears from this era tend to be found well worn.

### EMIL TOYS

This firm came into being late in the 1930s and manufactured their bears in Victoria.

❚ A main distinguishing feature of these bears was their pugnacious appearance due to their large, round, permanently fixed heads set close to the shoulders, small ears, wide-apart glass eyes, very distinctive broad noses with a pronounced upward elongated stitching, and long horizontal mouths.

ABOVE **This bear from Emil Toys, made in the late 1930s and measuring 40.5 cm/ 16 in, is recognizable by its fixed head.**

### JOY TOYS PTY

Australia's first teddy bear manufacturers were established in Melbourne in the late 1920s. But for some years they struggled until *circa* 1935 when they started to produce Disney characters.

❚ Joy Toys bears from this era used quality mohair and were usually softly filled with cotton flock except for the

ABOVE **This early Joy Toys bear from the 1930s, measuring 61 cm/24 in, is fully articulated unlike many other Australian bears. It closely resembles British bears from the same era.**

head, which used excelsior, occasionally this was also used for the rest of the bear.

❚ A label, sewn across the centre of the right foot rexine pad, was embroidered green on white "Joy-Toys made in Australia" (labels have also been found on the left foot).

❚ There is a close resemblance between Joy Toys and the Chiltern "Hugmee".

## FRANCE

Probably of all the bears made during this period, these are the most difficult to authenticate. Perhaps the most distinctive features were the rather primitive exposed metal rods used to attach limbs, and short bristly mohair. Probably because of their inferior quality and their unhappy looks, French bears have been of little interest to collectors. However, they are now beginning to attract attention.

### FADAP (1920)

Bears made by this firm (Fabrique Artistique d'Animaux en Peluche) are just beginning to appear and are recognizable by their distinctive red bordered tag, with a smaller overlapping circle at the bottom marked "FADAP", attached to the left ear with a metal button.

❚ This firm appeared to adopt the more conventional construction with concealed disc joints.

❚ The firm also produced teddy bears on wheels similar to Steiff's record series.

### M. PINTEL FILS AND CIE

Early in the 1920s they introduced bears.

❚ They used a small, round, moulded, brass-coloured button depicting two hugging bears and the letters "PF".

❚ Their bears had long tapering arms with long slender legs attached to a rather flat, almost shapeless body.

### THIENNOT (1919–20)

Another French firm who are supposed to have started manufacturing bears following World War I. However, little information currently exists regarding their bears.

## SWITZERLAND

### HELVETIC (MID-1920s)

Manufacture commenced in the mid-1920s but nobody can be quite sure about this maker's origins.

❚ The Helvetic range of musical bears are a must for any collector. The bears are quite distinctive, usually made of beautiful coloured long shaggy mohair with very appealing expressions.

❚ There is something rather American about these bears so perhaps Swiss musical boxes were shipped to the USA and inserted into locally made bears.

# POST-WAR RECOVERY (1946–60)

CHAPTER 3

Ravaged by the two world wars, disrupted by serious economic problems, many of the world's teddy bear manufacturers ceased to exist. A difficult time was in store for all the acknowledged quality toy manufacturers as they tried to pick up the pieces and re-establish themselves. They could not possibly foresee that within three decades the world would drastically change beyond all recognition as the new technological age and throw-away society evolved. No longer were children encouraged to nurture their beloved favourite toy – toys soon became plentiful and children less considerate and far more demanding for the very latest TV toy! Cheap goods were the prerequisite of the post-war baby boom.

It is surprising, therefore, that the most successful were the quality manufacturers such as Steiff, Schuco, Hermann, Chiltern and Chad Valley. Sadly, their success was short-lived as the multi-national conglomerate toy companies – usually American – just swallowed up all and sundry as they sought to control mass markets. No company was safe and all felt the threat of these big boys, as well as the threat of the continued rise of Japan as a major toy-producing nation.

To compound the problems for teddy bear manufacturers, the Americans introduced new stringent safety regulations in the late 1950s and these were soon to spread to other countries.

The teddy bears which followed from the mid-1950s right through to the 1970s were certainly soft and cuddly, made to conform to international safety standards, and above all, cheap.

LEFT **This wonderful Chad Valley teddy c. 1950 is bidding farewell to an old friend – a Steiff c. 1905.**

# COLLECTOR'S NOTEBOOK 1946–60

Unfortunately for collectors the new safety rules so profoundly affected and restricted the design and manufacture of teddy bears that after about 1960 they are generally lacking in character and appeal.

## USA

The mass-market conglomerates were starting to have their bears made in the cheap labour markets of the Far East. Inevitably the traditional teddy bear-makers found it difficult to compete.

### CHARACTER NOVELTY CO

The bears produced after the war and in the 1950s used the unusual technique of black button eyes applied to a white felt backing.

▌ This firm used a printed label bearing the name "Character" which appears to have been sewn into the bear's left ear.

### GUND INC (1906)

Gund made quite a variety of bears but they tended to concentrate on producing soft toys based on Disney characters. Consequently, few distinctive teddy bears were produced.

▌ Fortunately, precise names of each product were included on their labels which makes identification easy.

### IDEAL TOY AND NOVELTY CO (1903)

Like many of the post-war British manufacturers, the quality of bears produced by this famous firm had gradually diminished over the years. As they were now of course producing for the mass-market, this is not surprising.

▌ During the 1950s they produced a cute little teddy with moulded vinyl face, hands and feet. This theme was quite popular among American firms during this time.

### KNICKERBOCKER TOY CO

Like so many others, this popular American firm were producing bears based on their pre-war designs except that they now seemed to prefer the shaven inset muzzle rather like German firms. They produced some very nice good quality bears during the late 1940s and 1950s but little else.

RIGHT **This Knickerbocker bear from the 1940s (height 50 cm/20 in) is one of the best post-war American teddies. Note the label on the chest.**

LEFT **The notable features of Character Novelty Co bears of the late 1940s are the shape and the felt pads behind the eyes. (Height 49 cm/19½ in).**

## U K

### WENDY BOSTON (c. 1945)

Speak to anyone in the UK who are in their forties and they will probably tell you they were brought up on Wendy Boston bears produced during the 1950s and into the 1960s. The "Playsafe" nylon teddy could be thrown in the washing machine to emerge looking as good as new.

▌ These colourful one-piece bears came in all sizes and are now just beginning to be appreciated once again.

▌ Look for the bears with pinky white printed satin trademark, usually sewn into the sole of the right foot. Even if the bears had been washed many times you cannot mistake the label. Other manufacturers copied but their bears were not the same.

▌ During the early 1950s Wendy Boston also made conventional jointed mohair teddy bears. These would be a good find.

ABOVE **A representative range of Wendy Boston "Playsafe" bears from the late 1950s and 1960s. Note that some bears have their labels on the right foot, which is normal, and some on the left.**

### THE CHAD VALLEY CO LTD (1914)

Many of Chad's first bears after the war were based on the pre-war designs. Gradually the wonderful character faces were sadly replaced by flat-faced rather uninspiring teddy bears. Chad seemed to have lost their desire or perhaps ability to produce quality bears as the influence of the pre-war bears disappeared. With perhaps one or two exceptions Chad bears from this era do not attract much attention.

RIGHT **A Chad Valley bear from c. 1950 measuring 72 cm/28½ in. This bear has the earlier Royal Warrant which reads "HM the Queen". It was changed in 1953 to read "HM Queen Elizabeth the Queen Mother".**

### DEANS RAG BOOK CO LTD (1915)

A remarkable new line, based on real animals including a bear, was designed by Sylvia Wilgoss in 1955.

▌ Its moulded face was overcovered by mohair and it had moulded rubber hands and feet.

▌ There was a black bear and a white bear (supposed to be a polar bear) and both are very scarce.

### J.K. FARNELL & CO LTD (1908)

Almost the same can be said for Farnell except that some of the Farnell bears produced during early 1950s are worth seeking out. Look for the blue and red printed label with a shield which was attached to bears made from 1940 to 1964. In 1964 to coincide with the company moving to Hastings, Sussex, a plain printed label was used "This is a Farnell Quality Soft Toy made in Hastings, England". Unfortunately, the bears never really lived up to the slogan.

BELOW **A Deans bear from *c.* 1955 measuring 51 cm/20 in. The black versions of these "realistic" teddies are grizzly bears and the off-white ones, as here, polar bears.**

### MERRYTHOUGHT LTD (1930)

The firm continued with similar designs from the late 1930s but it really took the "Punkinhead" bear, followed by "Cheeky" to revive interest in Merrythought. Early versions of these particular bears should have the printed label with "Hygienic Toys" (centre) rather than the wording "Ironbridge, Shrops" which appeared from 1957 onwards.

### PEDIGREE SOFT TOYS LTD (1937)

This was the name of a range of soft toys produced under the banner of Lines Brothers from 1937.

▌ The quality varied from good to poor, but the distinctive feature was a nose placed high on the face with a long lip extending downwards to the mouth.

▌ The bears were made in the London suburb of Merton until 1955 when production was transferred to Northern Ireland.

▌ Plastic noses were used extensively in the late 1950s.

ABOVE **These are two bears from Merrythought's popular "Cheeky" range. Made in the late 1950s they measure 38 cm/15 in and 61 cm/24 in.**

RIGHT **This is probably the last real character bear produced by Farnells. The label on the side of the body fixes the date of this bear to 1964/5. The height of the bear is 45 cm/17½ in.**

### H.G. STONE & CO LTD (CHILTERN)

**(1920)** "Hugmee" bears still continued as the tour de force in the Chiltern range, and the 1950s bears are ones to look for.

▌ There were now facial changes with the introduction of the unshaven snout but the general body construction and shape remained very much the same.

▌ Printed labels, blue on white, were now glued on to the sole of the right foot. These often became detached but, if you look very carefully, you can usually see where they were.

▌ Red printed labels were also used on some teddy bears but these, along with similar style blue labels, were usually sewn into the seam at the side of the body.

▌ Plastic moulded noses were used *circa* 1958 and the ears then applied were vertical floppy style.

▌ Other favourites are the Ting-a-Ling Bear (1953) and the musical Baby Bruin (1958). These are rather similar bears except the latter had fixed legs to enable it to stand upright.

### OTHER BRITISH MANUFACTURERS

**ACTON TOY CRAFT LTD** Produced the Twyford range of bears which are really nice character bears but quite hard to find. Incidentally, Twyford bears often had red foot and hand pads.

**LECO TOYS** Whose bears are thought to be musical with a rather charming snub-nosed, upturned snout.

**LEFRAY LTD (1948)** Established in 1948 but moved to St Albans in 1960. Lefray bears were typically British for the period, except for a very unusual standing bear made with a fixed body and strange face.

RIGHT **A later (early 1960s) version of the Chiltern Hugmee, measuring 68 cm/27 in. The ears lie flat on the head and the face is slightly more pointed than before.**

ABOVE **This musical standing bear was made by Chiltern in 1959/60 and measures 29 cm/11½ in. The nose is moulded plastic.**

ABOVE **This Chiltern Hugmee was made c. 1956 and measures 53 cm/21 in. The basic shape of Hugmees had not changed.**

RIGHT **An unusual bear made by Lefray Ltd in the mid 1950s (height 53 cm/21 in). It is made to stand with very short fixed legs, but the head and arms are articulated. The ears are lined with brown velvet and the nostrils are red in colour.**

**S. OPPENHEIMER LTD** Produced teddy bears under the trademark "EMU" in 1950, distinguished by their triangular footpads.

**PLUMMER AND WANDLESS & CO LTD** Produced a range of teddy bears under the name of "Tinka-Bell".

**W.T. CO** Produced a soft-bodied clockwork teddy in 1951 that danced and walked, and another magic eye (battery-operated) bear. These bears also had triangular foot pads.

## GERMANY

### GEBRÜDER HERMANN (1911)

Hermann continued to make similar bears to those produced in pre-war times but they also introduced a "Zotty" style around the same time as Steiff.

▌ Although these "Zottys" appear the same, the formation of the nose and mouth is quite different, it does not have a coloured bib and the eyes do not have felt backgrounds.

▌ Perhaps more collectible are the two-tone mohair bears produced during the mid-1950s, which closely resemble those produced before the war.

▌ Look for the green and silver rosette-style hanging chest tag implemented in 1952, but if you find a bear with a circular pressed metal tag inscribed "Hermann – Teddy – Original", then you will know that bear was produced during the period 1941–51.

ABOVE **This popular bear by Gebrüder Hermann, made c. 1956 and measuring 41 cm/16 in, still has its green tag.**

ABOVE **This Gebr. Hermann bear is from c. 1953 and measures 30 cm/12 in. It may be hard to tell these apart from Steiffs.**

### SCHUCO (SCHREYER & CO) (1912)

Schucho bears made immediately after World War II are the most sought after of all those produced during Schuco's history.

❚ Without doubt the star of the Schuco range was a version of the "Yes-No" bear called "Tricky". There was also a musical version made of this bear. Look for one with its red rosette-style plastic chest tag inscribed "Schuco Tricky"; if it says "made in US Zone Germany" on the reverse side, this predates 1953.

❚ Another favourite, particularly if you can find her fully clothed, is the lovely "Yes-No" girl dressed in flowered frock and pinafore. Most notable is the fact that the head, hands and feet were made of mohair and attached to an excelsior-filled fabric body, arms and legs.

❚ Schuco also continued their range of metal-bodied miniatures; pre-war miniatures had felt feet applied but these were not used after the war except, we believe, on one very early 1950s bear.

LEFT **A Schuco bear c. 1950 measuring 44 cm/17½ in. Schuco kept up their pre-war standards but it is hard to find bears in such good condition.**

BELOW **This 1952 Steiff illustrates the gradual change in style between the late 1930s and the early 1950s. This bear measures 33 cm/13 in.**

BELOW **Steiff Zotties (l–r): 28 cm/11 in from 1956/7; 28 cm/11 in c. 1955; 28 cm/11 in c. 1970 and 22 cm/8½ in from the mid 1960s.**

### MARGARETE STEIFF (1903)

If you look closely at the immediate post-war teddy bears, you can clearly see the relationship with those produced ten or twenty years before. The slender faces are still quite distinctively Steiff but the new era demanded changes which even Steiff could not avoid.

▌ The 50th Anniversary bear produced in 1953 in three sizes called "Jackie" is likely to prove one of the best finds.

▌ The "Zotty" range of open-mouthed bears with their distinctive shaggy, frosted-tipped mohair and light-coloured chests were introduced in 1951. These are great fun to collect offering lots of variety but always try for those complete with ear tag and chest label.

▌ Beware, however, because there were many look-alikes produced by other makers.

▌ The rarest of all "Zotty's" is the white one.

▌ Derivatives of the "Zotty" were the "Zulac Zotty", "Orsi", "Lully" and "Zooby", made during the mid-1950s and well worth considering.

BELOW **A Steiff bear from 1954/5 measuring 28 cm/11 in. In 1952 the original Steiff design became a little more rotund.**

### OTHER GERMAN MANUFACTURERS

### HERMANN-SPIELWAREN GMBH (1920)

The Hermann-Speilwaren company was formerly known as Max Hermann & Sohn with premises in Sonneberg. In 1947 Max Hermann changed the name of the firm to the Hermann & Co Kg which had premises in both Sonneberg and Coburg 20 miles away. In 1953 Max moved the whole firm from Sonneberg (in the Russian occupied zone) to Coburg where they have remained ever since. They were not therefore two different Hermann firms! Look for the early two-tone tipped mohair bear model 73. The firm used a green triangular pressed metal tag with a walking bear and a dog as their trademark.

### PETZ COMPANY

There is much confusion and contradictory information about this company. Some authorities suggest the firm existed and were making bears as early as World War I while others suggest they commenced after World War II. As yet we cannot be sure. Most of the Petz bears you are likely to find can be positively identified if they have the distinctive white glass, red-lettered, round trademark tag fixed to the chest, and these are likely to be from about 1946 onwards.

▌ Other manufacturers known to have made bears during this period were: Clemens, Grisly Spielwaren, Althans KG, Anker, Baweku GmbH, Baumann & Kienel KG, EBO, Heunec and Hugo Koch.

## AUSTRALIA

### BERLEX TOY PTY (1930s)

Quite when this firm started making bears is not clear, although they had been in operation since the 1930s. We suspect it was probably some time in the 1950s because the bears are typical of that era employing cheaper quality mohair.

▌ They adopted the fixed head style which was popular among many Australian bear-makers.

▌ Look for the red printed on white label attached to either arm, and triangular stitched noses which Berlex favoured.

BELOW **The head on this 1950s Berlex bear is fixed but the limbs are articulated. Note the triangular nose and the label on the left arm. (Height 51 cm/20 in.)**

BELOW **A bear from the Australian company Emil Toys. It was made in the 1950s and measures 51 cm/20 in. Despite having only one eye, this fixed-head mohair bear will appeal to a great many collectors. Note the elongated outer stitching on the nose.**

RIGHT **This attractive bear was made *c.* 1960 and measures 70 cm/30 in. Although made from a woollen blend plush, it has a great character. Note the label on the right foot.**

### EMIL TOYS (LATE 1930S)

The bears made by this firm were remarkably similar to those made by Joy Toys, except Emil Toys bears always seem to lack any claw markings.

▌ Look for the label on the back or arm with a large letter "E" with a teddy bear on it.

### JAKAS (1954)

Based in Melbourne, Jakas commenced their bear-making in 1954. They made a wide variety of soft toys including teddy bears. They usually used a black printed on fawn-coloured silk label sewn on the right foot pad.

### JOY TOYS PTY (LATE 1920S)

Post-war Australian makers, including Joy Toys, still followed similar design concepts to the British.

▌ Although mohair had been extensively used, it was now replaced more and more by cheap synthetic plushes. The soft cotton flock filling was also dropped in favour of synthetic foam filling. The problem with the latter is it deteriorates and crumbles easily.

▌ Both the elongated, outer stitched nose and the green printed on white label were retained in post-war production by Joy Toys.

BELOW **A typical Australian bear from Jorg Toys. Made in the 1960s and measuring 38 cm/15 in, it is filled with foam rubber.**

### LINDEE TOYS (LATE 1940s)

Established in Sydney during the late
war years, they produced a variety of
typically Australian teddy bears.

▌ During their early period they made a
rather attractive musical bear with a
distinctive moulded rubber nose and
unusual teardrop-shaped rexine pads.

▌ A trademark was sewn to the right foot
with an unusual red painted on white
seated deer with the words "Lindee
Toys" inscribed inside.

Other manufacturers known to have
made bears during this period were L.J.
Sterne Doll Co of East Malvern,
Victoria, and Parker Toys of Brunswick,
Victoria.

### VERNA (LATE 1940s)

Although this firm was established in
1941, it seems highly likely that due to
wartime trade restrictions they did not
start manufacturing bears until around
1948.

▌ Verna bears have a strong British
influence but look for the nose made of
pieces of kidney-shaped felt.

▌ Foam rubber moulding techniques
were used for the heads, bodies and
limbs, to which the fabric was applied.

▌ Verna bears were marked by a red
embroidered on white label.

### OTHER MANUFACTURERS

**BERG** This Austrian bear-maker began
immediately after World War II and
marked their bears with a label sewn into
the ear on the body reading "BERG".
Later this was changed to a red heart-
shaped trademark sewn into the chest.

**FETCHER** Immediately after World War
II this firm commenced manufacture in
Graz, Austria and an open-mouthed bear
was a prominent feature of their range.
Easily distinguishable by their very large
round heads, inset snouts and very large
ears placed at the top of the heads which
usually had different coloured lined
inner ears. The Fetcher label was sewn
on to the outside of the bear's right ear.
Quite often red-coloured eyes appear to
have been used.

**MUTZI (M.C.Z.)** This Swiss firm based in
Zurich made a wide range of teddy bears
which are very like German bears in
appearance. They used a round metal
button with the emblem of a teddy bear
with "Mutzi M.C.Z." on a red painted
base. So far as we can tell, Felpa AG and
Mutzi were one and the same company.

ABOVE **An appealing bear from
Lindee Toys, made in the 1950s
and measuring 51 cm/20 in.
Note the moulded rubber nose
and tear-shaped rexine foot
pads.**

RIGHT **This foam-filled Verna
bear was made in the 1950s and
measures 76 cm/30 in. Note
the kidney-shaped black felt
nose and embroidered mouth.**

# THE AGE OF SPECIAL EDITION BEARS

## CHAPTER 4

After nearly two decades – the 1960s and 1970s – when very few bears of serious interest to collectors were produced, 1980 marked the start of a new and exciting era. It was Margarete Steiff GmbH which was again to dominate, reaffirming its position as the leading manufacturer of quality soft toys and teddy bears.

LEFT **One of the best contemporary Steiffs – the first of the British Collector's series is a 1989 replica of a 1907 bear (height 61 cm/24 in).**

ABOVE **This is a full set of the delightful 1909 replicas issued by Steiff between 1983 and 1988. The smaller and larger bears were issued only to the USA.**

RIGHT **A wonderful mohair bear by Little Folk from 1982 measuring 56 cm/22 in was only produced for about 2 years. It is also available in 30 cm/12 in.**

# MANUFACTURERS SPECIALIZING IN LIMITED EDITIONS

## USA

### BEARLY THERE INC (1976)

Started in 1976 by Linda Spiegel Lohre, the original bears were rather traditional but since *circa* 1985 the bears have shown a close affinity to the "Artist"-type bear. Bearly There bears continue to be extremely popular all over the world.

### NORTH AMERICAN BEAR CO (1979)

Barbara Isenberg created this company in 1979 but the introduction of the Very Important Bear range (V.I.B.) in 1980 was what really caught the collector's eye. Based on famous celebrities, the range included Amelia Bearheart, Abearheim Lincoln, Bearlie Chaplin, Bearilyn Monroe and Elizabear Taylor with Richard Bearton, based on the film *Cleopawtra*.

▌ In 1983, they produced an edition of "Hug", the famous character bear by Ted Menten.

▌ Another hugely successful range was the "Vanderbear" series and the "Muffy" series.

▌ Initially preferred by American collectors, these bears are now appreciated in other parts of the world.

### ROBERT RAIKES ORIGINALS (1982)

These charming and funny little bears are quite distinctive with their wooden character faces.

▌ The first bears were produced by Robert Raikes' own hands in 1982, but since around 1984 all his design creations have been manufactured by Applause.

▌ The pre-Applause bears are among the most sought after of all contemporary bears and Raikes has a tremendous following. However, those first Applause made bears are also much in demand (the first edition of 7,500 was sold out in three weeks).

▌ Of the original bears made by Raikes' own hands the first one is simply called "Woody Bear" and subsequent designs – "Panda Woody Bear" and "Tyrone Woody Bear" (Scotsman) – are the most in demand and rather expensive.

▌ The first series, limited to 7,500 each and issued in Autumn 1985 by Applause, comprised Sebastian (5445), Huckle Bear (5446), Rebecca (5447), Bentley (5448), Eric (5449) and Chelsea (5551).

## UK

### CANTERBURY BEARS (1981)

John and Maude Blackburn commenced serious manufacturing of bears in 1981 and have grown from a small family group to a medium-sized company. Canterbury have produced large quantities of standard range bears in addition to limited editions especially for collectors, all of which are handmade by a loyal and dedicated workforce.

▌ The Blackburns are great favourites on the American personal appearance circuit. Since 1991, they have collaborated with Gund Inc of America to make a very special range of collectible limited editions for the USA.

RIGHT **"Hug", from the North American Bear Co,** was designed by Ted Menten and measures 47 cm/18 in. It was one of their earliest successes – *c.* 1983.

ABOVE **"Rosie" by Canterbury Bears** was made in 1993. She was designed by Maude and John Blackburn, two leading designers of both special editions and standard ranges. She measures 53 cm/21 in.

ABOVE **Canterbury Bear's 10th anniversary bear (100/500) from 1991 (58 cm/23 in) embraces the special edition "Swallow" (1/25) made in 1993 (60 cm/ 24 in).**

## DEANS RAG BOOK CO LTD (1915)
### (NOW THE DEANS COMPANY (1903))

This is another British company which realized the importance of the collectors' market, when in 1981 they produced bears for the USA based on Norman Rockwell drawings. They have continued to manufacture collectible bears and in the past few years their range has substantially improved.

## LITTLE FOLK (1980)

From the outset in 1980 Little Folk realized there was greater potential in the USA where most of their bears were exported. Their very early designs used mohair but this meant the bears were probably too expensive and cheaper acrylic plush was successfully introduced *circa* 1982. This same range is produced today and much in demand.
▌ A 2,000 limited edition bear Sebastian (1987) and 500 No Jonathon's (1990) have also been produced with collectors in mind. We have a special place in our hearts for Little Folk bears because these were the first contemporary bears we ever sold.

## MERRYTHOUGHT LTD (1930)

In 1982 Merrythought decided to introduce a range of limited edition bears, usually based on their old designs, for the USA market. Recently several new designs have been added, including those inspired by John Axe (author of *The Magic of Merrythought*) and others based on the drawings of the English illustrator, Prue Theobalds.

LEFT **This attractively costumed plush bear "heading for the hills" was the result of a collaboration between Lakeland Bears, who designed the outfits, and Little Folk *c.* 1991. The bear measures 60 cm/ 23½ in.**

## HOUSE OF NISBET (1978)

Of all the contemporary manufacturers, the House of Nisbet under the leadership of Jack Wilson were probably the most adventurous. He cultivated an extremely fruitful business relationship with the amazing Peter Bull, resulting in the introduction of the "Bully Bear" range, and the delightful edition of 12 "Zodiac" bears, based on a book by Pauline McMillan and Peter Bull. It was a very great loss to the teddy bear world when Jack decided to retire in 1989 and the House of Nisbet was taken over by Dakin.
▌ "Delicatessen" ("Aloysius"), another of Peter Bull's bears, is without equal and incidentally was directly responsible for the introduction of distressed mohair which artists have since found so helpful.

ABOVE **"Delicatessan" (number 1031 of 2500) from the House of Nisbet, *c.* 1987, measuring 63 cm/25 in. This limited edition is now rather hard to find and is a must for any collector.**

## THE NISBET CELEBRITY
## COLLECTION

**Hedda Hair bear from 1989 (40 cm/16 in).**

The following bears, produced in the Nisbet Celebrity Collection, were limited to 5,000 of each design.

Yetta bear, Eric-Jon bear, Maybe and Wizard, all by Carol-Lynn Rössell Waugh ● Little Brown bear by Johnny Gruelle ● Pearly King bear by Doris and Terry Michaud ● Uncle Wiggily by Mabel R. Garis ● The Bell Hop bear and The Clown bear by April Whitcomb ● Yes-No bear, based on the Schuco method ● Sir Freddie Farthing by Ted Menten ● Precious the Paper Doll bear by Peggy Jo Rosamond ● Mr Do-it-all bear by Linda Mullins ● The Hedda Hair bear by Lillian Rohaly ● The Anything bear by Rosemary Volpp ● Theodore B. Bear and Victoria Bear, both by Beverley Port ● Red Mittens bear by Pat Schoonmaker ● Grinnee Bearit by Lucy Major ● Gyles bear by Gyles Brandreth ● Drum Major bear by Dee Hockenberry ● and Bentley bear by Dakin.

Although listed in Nisbet's 1990 catalogue, the Jim Ownby Tribute bear by Peggy Maxwell was apparently never produced.

▌ The "Nisbet Celebrity" collection was an inspired move by the astute Jack who had been quick to realize that there were other "celebrities" in the rapidly expanding Teddy Bear collecting fraternity. In 1987 he invited well-known people to have a bear made in their name or asked artists to design a special bear.

## GERMANY

### GEBRÜDER HERMANN (1911)
This small family firm, consistently one of Germany's mainstream producers, entered the new specialist production market in 1984. Like many other established firms, they have produced bears based on their earlier designs that have been well received by collectors worldwide.

▌ The "Anniversary" bear (1986), "Designer" bear (1991), "Berlin Wall" bear (1991) and "Unification" bear (1991) are perhaps the best-known.

ABOVE. **A limited edition replica of a 1930s bear from Gebrüder Hermann. It was issued to commemorate Helen Sieverling's efforts to expand teddy bear collectors' knowledge.**

BELOW **The "Designer" bear, 1991, measuring 57 cm/23 in, shows the character and quality of the limited edition bears produced by Gebrüder Hermann.**

**MARGARETE STEIFF (1903)**

Spurred on by the need for a fresh approach to fight off the threat of cheap imports, Steiff introduced a special edition teddy bear in 1980 to commemorate the 100th anniversary of the company. Its success enabled them to implement state of the art production methods to reproduce the originals kept in the Steiff museum, which had also opened that year, as faithfully as possible, modern materials permitting.

▌ Steiff regularly made exclusive limited editions for major department stores worldwide and also produced editions for Disney World and Disneyland Conventions held annually in the USA.

▌ Many, but by no means all, of the Steiff replica bears have appreciated in value, some substantially, which may be an inducement to some collectors.

▌ So many special limited editions of bears have been issued that a reference chart of those produced by Steiff until 1993 is given on page 45. Only limited editions carrying white tags have been included. Although some absolutely wonderful yellow tag (standard production) bears were produced, it is impossible to list them too.

▌ Many of the yellow tags are highly collectible and some can be rather expensive; perhaps the most desirable are the early "Mr Cinnamon" bears made in three sizes and the "Margaret Strong" bears produced in the mid-1980s.

RIGHT **The larger Steiff bear from 1993 produced as a limited edition of 5000 (70 cm/ 28 in).**

BELOW **Steiff's 1990 replica of the world famous "Happy", looking as she would have done when new in 1926. She measures 65 cm/26 in.**

BELOW **One of five sizes of (unlimited) "Margaret Strong" gold bears introduced by Steiff in 1982. (60 cm/23½ in).**

## STEIFF LIMITED EDITION TEDDY BEARS

ABOVE **"Jubilee" or "Papa" bear was the first modern limited edition, produced in 1980 (height 43 cm/17 in).**

### KEY TO SCARCITY FACTOR

| | |
|---|---|
| **1–3** | currently available and easy to find |
| **4–5** | moderately easy to find |
| **6–8** | relatively difficult to find |
| **9–10** | very rare and expensive |

NOTE: Until 1991, the last two numbers of the product code indicate size in cm. The EAN number, a European standard, was then introduced.

N/A = not applicable    W/W = worldwide

| YEAR OF PRODUCTION | | REPLICA PRODUCT CODE | DESCRIPTION | QUANTITY | SCARCITY FACTOR |
|---|---|---|---|---|---|
| ORIGINAL | REPLICA | | | | |
| 1903 | 1980 | 0153/43 | JUBILEE BEAR, but commonly known as PAPA BEAR | 11,000 W/W (6,000 German certificate, 5,000 to USA, English certificate) | 9–10 |
| 1903 | 1981 | 0155/38 | MAMA and BABY SET (Mama 40 cm/16 in, Baby 15 cm/6 in) | 8,000 USA | 9 |
| N/A | 1982 | 0203/00 | ORIGINAL TEDDY WHITE SET | 2,000 USA | 9 |
| N/A | 1982 | 0204/17 | TEA PARTY SET (4 dressed bears with tea set and scene) | 10,000 USA | 6–7 |
| 1905 | 1982/83 | 0150/32 | RICHARD STEIFF GREY TEDDY BEAR | Unnumbered No certificate but tied-on booklet is signed. Estimates vary from 11,000 to 20,000 W/W | 8 |
| N/A | 1983 | 0210/22 | TEDDY ROOSEVELT COMMEMORATIVE SET or NIMROD or CAMP FIRE (4 small dressed bears with scene) | 10,000 USA (Note: many sets were broken up and bears sold separately) | 7 |
| 1904 | 1983 | 0160/00 | MARGARET STRONG CHOCOLATE SET (4 different bears 18 cm/7 in, 26 cm/10½ in, 32 cm/12¾ in and 42 cm/17 in) | 2,000 USA | 8 |

RIGHT **The "Circus Dolly" bear, issued in 1987, was made in four colours. It was first distributed in the USA, followed by the rest of the world.**

LEFT **"Dicky" was produced in 1985 in a very large limited edition of 20,000, but its collectibility is now increasing (height 32 cm/13 in).**

RIGHT **The delightful "Teddy Clown" was made in 1986 and measures 32 cm/13 in. As with all Steiff collector's bears, it is handmade from the finest quality mohair.**

ABOVE **This small grey "Richard Steiff" was made in 1982/3 and measures 32 cm/ 13 in. It was based on Richard Steiff's prototype and is a great favourite with collectors.**

| YEAR OF PRODUCTION | | REPLICA PRODUCT CODE | DESCRIPTION | QUANTITY | SCARCITY FACTOR |
|---|---|---|---|---|---|
| ORIGINAL | REPLICA | | | | |
| 1904 | 1984 | 0156/00 | MARGARET STRONG CINNAMON SET (4 different bears 18 cm/ 7 in, 26 cm/10½ in, 32 cm/ 12¾ in and 42 cm/17 in) | 2,000 USA | 8–9 |
| 1894 | 1984 | 0082/20 | ROLY-POLY BEAR | 9,000 W/W | 4–5 |
| 1906 | 1984 | 0162/00 | GIENGEN TEDDY SET (Mother 32 cm/12½ in with Baby in Cradle 10 cm/4 in) | 16,000 W/W | 6–7 |
| N/A | 1984 | 4003 (Large Set) | GOLDILOCKS & 3 BEARS Papa Bear 33 cm/13 in, Mama 30 cm/12 in, Baby 24 cm/9½ in. Doll by Susan Gibson | 2,000 USA | 7 |
| N/A | 1984 | 0225/42 | OPHELIA BEAR from *Ophelia's World* by Michelle Durkson-Clise | USA Limited by time production (Note: Button but no tag) | 7 |
| 1930 | 1985 | 0172/32 | DICKY BEAR | 20,000 W/W | 6 |
| 1905 | 1985 | 0085/12 | BEAR ON WHEELS | 12,000 W/W | 5 |
| N/A | 1985 | 4004 (Smaller Set) | GOLDILOCKS & 3 BEARS Papa Bear 23 cm/9 in, Mama 18 cm/7 in, Baby 12.5 cm/ 5 in and doll | 5,000 USA | 6–7 |
| 1904 | 1985 | 0158/25  0158/31 0158/41 | MARGARET STRONG WHITE (leather pads) (leather pads) (leather pads) | 2,000 USA | 8 |
| 1904 | 1986 | 0158/50 | MARGARET STRONG WHITE (leather pads) Large | 750 USA | 9–10 |
| 1926 | 1986 | 0170/32 | TEDDY CLOWN | 10,000 W/W | 7 |
| 1953 | 1986/7 | 0190/25 | JACKIE BEAR (medium-size) | 10,000 W/W | 6–7 |
| 1913 | 1987 | 0164/31 0164/32 0164/33 0164/30 | CIRCUS DOLLY BEARS yellow green violet pale yellow (Note: blue and red also shown in catalogue but not produced) | 5,000 USA initially, then W/W | 6–7 6 6 9 |

BELOW **"Teddy Rose"**, a centre seam replica, was made in 1987 and measures 41 cm/16 in and has many fans among collectors.

RIGHT **"Jackie"**, a reproduction of the 1953 anniversary bear, was first made in 1988 and is shown here in all the sizes so far issued.

| YEAR OF PRODUCTION | | REPLICA PRODUCT CODE | DESCRIPTION | QUANTITY | SCARCITY FACTOR |
|---|---|---|---|---|---|
| ORIGINAL | REPLICA | | | | |
| 1905 | 1987 | 0163/19 | TEDDY CLOWN JR | 3,000 USA with white tags (Note: 2,000 also issued with yellow tags) | 8–9 |
| 1925 | 1987 | 0171/41 | TEDDY ROSE | 10,000 W/W | 6–7 |
| 1907 | 1987 | 0227/33 | SCHNUFFY | Limited by time production issued to USA but later about 300 released into UK (undresssed) (Note: Button no tag) | 7 |
| N/A | 1987 | 0131/00 | THREE BEARS IN A TUB butcher, baker and candle-stick maker in tub | 1,800 USA | 7–8 |
| N/A | 1988 | 0227/33 | BABY OPHELIA | Unstated limit USA. Only *Button* in ear | 6 |
| N/A | 1988 | 0120/10 | BEAR BANDSMAN (Circus series) | 5,000 USA | 5–6 |

| Year of Production Original | Replica | Replica Product Code | Description | Quantity | Scarcity Factor |
|---|---|---|---|---|---|
| 1953 | 1988 | 0190/35 | Jackie Bear (large) | 4,000 W/W | 5–6 |
| 1908 | 1988 | 0155/18 | Roly-Poly Bear | 3,000 USA | 7 |
| 1908 | 1988 | 0174/46 | White Muzzle Bear (medium-size) | 5,000 USA | 7–8 |
| 1907 | 1988 | 0173/40 | Black Bear (with leather nose) | 4,000 W/W | 8–9 |
| 1924 | 1988 | 0132/24 | 'Wig-Wam' Bear 2 small bears and pull-along seesaw | 4,000 W/W | 5–6 |
| 1907 | 1989 | 0174/61 | British Collectors Series Bear (1st) | 2,000 UK | 9–10 |
| 1939 | 1989 | 0135/20 | Baby Bear on Trolley | 4,000 W/W | 4–5 |
| 1931 | 1989 | 0130/28 | Bear on All Fours | 4,000 USA | 6 |
| 1908 | 1989 reissued 1991 (USA) | 0158/17 | Snap-a-Part Bear | 5,000 W/W | 5–6 |
| N/A | 1989 | 0175/19 | Teddy Bear Ringmaster | 7,000 USA | 4–5 |
| N/A | 1989 | 0163/20 | Clown Teddy From golden age of the circus series | 5,000 USA | 5 |

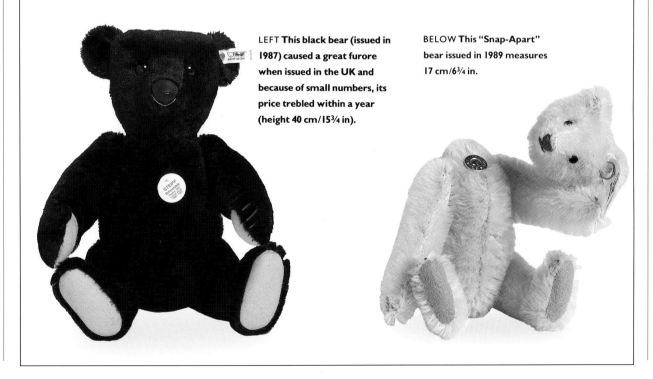

LEFT **This black bear (issued in 1987) caused a great furore when issued in the UK and because of small numbers, its price trebled within a year (height 40 cm/15¾ in).**

BELOW **This "Snap-Apart" bear issued in 1989 measures 17 cm/6¾ in.**

LEFT **The "Petsy Brass" replica was issued in 1989 and measures 35 cm/13¾ in.**

RIGHT **This is the reproduction of the blue "Bi-colour Petsy" issued in 1989. It measures 50 cm/19¾ in.**

| YEAR OF PRODUCTION | | REPLICA PRODUCT CODE | DESCRIPTION | QUANTITY | SCARCITY FACTOR |
|---|---|---|---|---|---|
| ORIGINAL | REPLICA | | | | |
| 1927 | 1989 | 0181/35 | PETSY BRASS | 5,000 W/W | 6 |
| 1953 | 1989 | 0190/17 | JACKIE BEAR | 12,000 W/W | 4 |
| 1927 | 1989 | 0180/50 | BICOLOR PESTY CENTRE SEAM | 5,000 USA | 6–7 |
| 1908 | 1989 | 0174/60 | WHITE MUZZLE BEAR (large) | 2,650 USA | 9–10 |
| 1908 | 1990 | 0174/35 | WHITE MUZZLE BEAR (small) | 6,000 W/W | 5 |
| 1926 | 1990 | 0169/65 | HAPPY ANNIVERSARY REPLICA | 5,000 W/W | 8–9 |
| 1925 | 1990 | 0171/25 | TEDDY ROSE (small) | 8,000 W/W | 5 |
| N/A | 1990 | 0177/19 | TEDDY BABY FOOD VENDOR (Circus series) | 5,000 USA | 4–5 |
| 1955 | 1990 | 0188/25 | TEDDY WITH NECK MECHANISM | 4,000 W/W | 5–6 |
| 1909 | 1990 | 0164/29 | SOMERSAULT BEAR | 5,000 W/W | 6–7 |
| 1906 | 1990 | 0174/33 | BRITISH COLLECTORS SERIES BEAR (No 2) | 3,000 UK | 5–6 |
| 1913 | 1990 | 0116/25 | RECORD TEDDY (on wheels) | 4,000 W/W | 7–8 |
| N/A | 1991 | 650529 (EAN) | TEDDY BABY TICKET SELLER (Circus series) | 5,000 USA | 4–5 |
| 1903 | 1991 | 404108 (EAN) | 35 PB REPLICA (50 cm/20 in) (in USA often referred to as "Baerle" bear) | 6,000 W/W | 8 |

| Year of Production | | EAN Numbers Used | Description | Quantity | Scarcity Factor |
|---|---|---|---|---|---|
| Original | Replica | | | | |
| 1926 | 1991 | 407215 | Baby Happy Anniversary (40 cm/16 in) (Note: Box incorrectly states 5,000 limit but certificate is correct) | 6,000 W/W | 4–5 |
| 1912 | 1991 | 406096 | British Collectors Series Black Bear (No 3) (33 cm/13 in) | 3,000 UK | 5–6 |
| 1908 | 1991 | 406119 | Dark Brown Muzzle (35 cm/14 in) | 5,000 USA | 4–5 |
| 1913 | 1991 | 400704 | Record Teddy Rose (on wheels) | 4,000 W/W | 3–4 |
| 1931 | 1991 | 408113 | Yellow Teddy Baby (15 cm/6 in) | 5,000 USA | 4 |
| 1931 | 1991 | 408114 | Yellow Teddy Bear (32 cm/12½ in) | 5,000 USA (a few later released to UK) | 4 |
| N/A | 1991 | 650529 | Teddy Baby Ticket Seller (Circus series) | 5,000 USA | 4 |
| 1930s | 1991 | 606106 | Teddy Baby Watch Set (1st Issue – complete stand, bear and 13 watches) | 2,000 W/W | 8 Complete Set |
| 1930s | 1992 | 606304 | Teddy Baby Watch Set (2nd Issue – complete stand, bear and 13 watches) | 4,000 W/W | 6–7 |

LEFT **This group of white muzzled bears was issued between 1988 and 1990. The larger of these (60 cm/23½ in) is extremely hard to find. The other sizes are 35 cm/13¾ in and 46 cm/18 in. Most collectors remove the muzzles.**

RIGHT **The 35PB replica was issued in 1991. It reproduces the string joints and sealing wax nose (height 50 cm/19½ in).**

BELOW **This somersault or "Purzel" bear was issued in 1990 and measures 29 cm/ 11½ in. It uses a clockwork mechanism.**

LEFT **The British Collector's series always produces attractive bears. This brown bear was issued in 1993 (height 60 cm/24 in).**

RIGHT **Another in the British Collector's series issued in 1992 and measuring 40 cm/16 in.**

| YEAR OF PRODUCTION | | EAN NUMBERS USED | DESCRIPTION | QUANTITY | SCARCITY FACTOR |
|---|---|---|---|---|---|
| ORIGINAL | REPLICA | | | | |
| 1911 | 1992 | 406645 | BRITISH COLLECTORS SERIES WHITE BEAR (No 4) (Sometimes referred to as LOUISE in the UK) (40 cm/16 in) | 3,000 UK | 4–5 |
| 1928 | 1992 | 407482 | YELLOW MUSICAL BEAR (40 cm/16 in) | 8,000 W/W | 3–4 |
| 1930 | 1992 | 407550 | WHITE DICKY BEAR (25 cm/10 in) | 9,000 W/W | 3 |
| 1930 | 1992 | 407574 | WHITE DICKY BEAR (33 cm/13 in) | 7,000 W/W | 3 |
| 1912 | 1992 | 406805 | SMALL BLACK BEAR (40 cm/16 in) | 7,000 W/W | 3–4 |
| 1912 | 1992 | 406774 | "OTTO" 1ST ISSUE NEW USA COLLECTORS SPECIAL (40 cm/16 in) | 5,000 USA | 3–4 |
| 1974 | 1992 | 400872 | SEESAW BEAR AND MONKEY (on wheels) | 4,000 W/W | 3 |
| N/A | 1992 | 038006 (WO38006) | NOAH'S ARK WITH MR AND MRS NOAH (20 cm/8 in) BEARS WITH BAMBOO ARK (Note: Wooden ark alternative offered in USA) | 8,000 W/W | 4 |
| 1905 | 1993 | 404207 | BARLE 35 PAB (35 cm/14 in) | 6,000 W/W | 3–4 |
| 1926 | 1993 | 400919 | UR TEDDY (20 cm/8 in) | 4,000 W/W | 1 |

| Year of Production | | EAN Numbers Used | Description | Quantity | Scarcity Factor |
| Original | Replica | | | | |
|---|---|---|---|---|---|
| 1951 | 1993 | 408458 | Musical Teddy (35cm/14 in) | 5,000 W/W | 2 |
| 1907 | 1993 | 406010 | Teddy Bear Brown 1907 (70 cm/28 in) | 5,000 W/W | 4–5 |
| 1930 | 1993 | 407512 | Teddy Baby Dressed Girl | 7,000 W/W | 1 |
| 1930 | 1993 | 407529 | Teddy Baby Dressed Boy | 2,000 W/W | 1 |
| 1907 | 1993 | 406065 | British Collectors Series Large Brown (No 5) (60 cm/24 in) | 3,000 W/W | 4 |
| 1903 | 1993 | 650574 | Alice 2nd Issue USA Special Collectors Series | 5,000 W/W | 3 |
| N/A | 1993 | 038327 | Bear Set for Ark Series (2 bears) | 8,000 W/W | 2 |
| 1929 | 1992/93 | 420016 | Steiff 1st Issue Club Bear Blue Teddy Baby (28 cm/11 in) | approx 7,500 issued outside USA | Available only to Steiff Collector Club members |
| N/A | 1993/94 | 420023 | Steiff 2nd Issue Club Bear Teddy Clown (28 cm/11 in) | issued outside USA | Available only to Steiff Collector Club members |
| N/A | 1993/94 | 420801 | Steiff USA 1st Issue Club Bear – Sam | issued only in USA | Available only to Steiff Collector Club members USA only |

LEFT **The first USA Steiff Collector's Club issue in 1994 was a bear called "Sam" (height 28 cm/11 in).**

RIGHT **The European Collector's Club was introduced in 1993 and has been a huge success. The "Blue Teddy Baby" (28 cm/11 in) was an exclusive issue to club members.**

The trouble in trying to define the term "teddy bear artist" is that this is such a contentious and emotive subject, you inevitably alienate some people. Probably above all else the major feature which distinguishes the real teddy bear artist from all other crafts people or bear-makers, is the ability to create, without the conscious influence of others, a teddy bear of distinctive quality and character. It is not just a matter of good workmanship, however desirable this may be; the design concept must be original with a clear aesthetic quality and style.

Many people are perfectly competent bear-makers and their workmanship is consistent and precise, but they are simply incapable of instilling life in a bear, or,

LEFT **Deborah Canham is one of Britain's best artists. These delightful circus bears (5 cm/ 2 in) were made in 1993.**

RIGHT **Jo Greeno created "Miss Marple", based on Agatha Christie's famous detective, in 1993 (height 48 cm/19 in). Jo specializes in interesting characters from the past. They are usually kept to small limited editions or are one-off designs.**

# THE ERA OF THE TEDDY BEAR ARTIST

LEFT **"Wizard" by Brenda Dewey (USA)** *c.* **1993. He measures 13 cm/5 in and is typical of her Fantasy style. Diverse in size and inspiration, these bears are usually limited editions or one-offs.**

CHAPTER 5

LEFT "Lady Margaret" was made by one of America's top artists, Marcia Sibol, in 1991 (height 84 cm/33 in) especially for the authors. She is the gossip columnist of the *Teddy Bear Times*!

RIGHT **Diane Gard (USA)** based "Billy Ray" on an American football hero. He was made exclusively for the 1992 Walt Disney World Doll and Teddy Bear Convention.

ABOVE **Janet Clark has been making bears seriously for three years and is now one of Britain's top artists. "Loving" was made in 1994.**

RIGHT **"Bearlin the White Wizard" by Kathryn Riley was created in 1993. Amazingly, he was only her third bear!**

as our old friend Steve Schutt often says, "giving the bear a soul". An artist bear must be instantly recognizable as the work of a particular creator, just as most people can easily distinguish the work of, say, Van Gogh from a painting by old Aunt Mabel!

All artists have to be innovators, otherwise their work becomes mundane, rather than inspirational and a teddy that we simply must own. A true teddy bear artist will possess a wide-ranging repertoire, be adventurous and not afraid to disregard convention, and instinctively be able to produce everything from classical to whimsical and even occasionally unusual designs. The artist will seek out new materials, apply new techniques or concepts, and constantly diversify his or her designs, rarely being perfectly content with the result.

Where did bear artistry begin? The true origins of the teddy bear artist are somewhat obscure, although we only have to go back to the 1970s in the USA to find who were the guiding spirits and true pioneers of the movement.

Many of the early craft bear-makers and their successors were largely influenced by two English people. One was Margaret Hutchings, a journalist on one of the UK's leading newspapers, who in 1964 wrote the definitive teddy bear-making manual, *The Book of the Teddy Bear*. The other was of course Peter Bull.

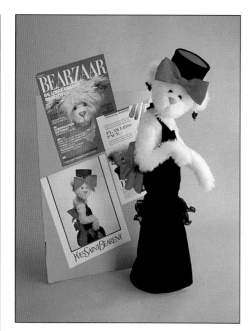

LEFT "Marisa Bearensen" was made by Diane Gard in 1988 (height 60 cm/24 in). She was created for Ted Menten's parody of *Harper's Bazaar*. "Marisa" is dressed in her Yves St Bearant gown.

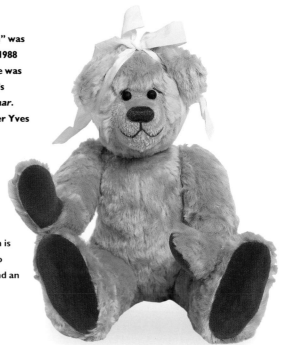

RIGHT "Jenny-Lynn" was made by Carol-Lynn Rössel Waugh (USA) in 1993 (height 50 cm/20 in). Carol-Lynn is a top artist in addition to being a prolific writer and an authority on teddy bear artistry. She has also designed bears for manufacturers.

The first teddy bear artist was the American, Beverley Port. From the 1970s Beverley guided and taught many of the current teddy bear artists. She had broken free from the traditional restraints and prejudices which had restricted her as a doll artist to pursue her new interest in teddy bear-making, encouraging a great many others by her example. She is recognized as the "mother" of teddy bear artistry.

In 1980, the Americans, Alan and Peggy Bialosky produced their book *Teddy Bears Catalogue* which provided added impetus and stimulus to those involved with teddy bears.

Carol-Lynn Rössell Waugh, herself an ex-doll maker, was one of the early disciples of this new movement. An art historian, she became a prominent authority on the subject and was probably the person who coined the term "teddy bear artist". She has written extensively over the years, promoting the work of artists, and has herself produced many fine bears, as well as designing for major manufacturers.

Another artist who was an undoubted inspiration and influence on the movement, not least because of his own designs, was Ted Menten. A photographer and author, his many wonderful teddy bear books have inspired others. His outrageous parody of *Harpers Bazaar* entitled *Teddy's Bearzaar* provided a unique opportunity for the invited artists to make special bears displaying their tremendous flair. The bears replaced the usual female models in the advertisements and articles to provide an absolutely wonderful, whimsical and funny book that has helped to open new horizons and, most importantly, validate artists and their bears as a highly collectible commodity.

ABOVE "Elfinbeary Peach" (14/100) illustrates Joan Woessner's versatility and creativity and confirms her position as a top American artist (1992).

LEFT **Anne Cranshaw's (USA)** "Casco Bear" (1993, 37 cm/14½ in) is a captivating little bear created for *Teddies of the World '93*.

RIGHT **"Bear and his Friend Grin it"** was made by **Karin and Howard Calvin (USA)** as a limited edition (1988, height 38 cm/15 in).

Around 1982–3 in the USA many aspiring people became attracted to bear-making, and some with undoubted qualities began to emerge and develop their skills. Teddy bear shows were also being established which gave prominence to a new generation of bear-makers – real artists who brought to the art not only new and invigorating design concepts but a positive desire to create an artistic group or community. Among the many who became idealistically involved were Steve Schutt, Diane Gard, Joan Woessner, Anne Cranshaw and Denis Shaw, who by their example epitomized integrity and strong ethical principles which bear artists were to find invaluable in the years ahead.

The foundations were laid for these instigators, and others, to encourage the sharing of ideas, knowledge and interaction with those of similar interests. The

ABOVE **Denis Shaw (USA)** brings to his designs his concerns for environmental issues and "Ursus", made in 1991, captures all the grace and ferocity of wild animals.

LEFT **"Antique Gray Bear"** was made by **Barbara Conley (USA)** in 1993 using traditional style and methods (height 39 cm/15½ in).

RIGHT **Dee Hockenberry (USA)**, creator of "Mr Bruin" (1990, height 37 cm/13 in), is one of the world's leading authorities on old bears in addition to being a talented artist.

ABOVE **Betsy Reum's (USA) "Puppeteer"** was made in 1987 as part of a limited edition of 100 bears. She produces exciting and varied designs that are highly collectible.

ABOVE **"Buster" by Brian Beacock (UK) was** made in 1987 and measures 50 cm/20 in. **Dr Brian is probably better known as a** teddy bear restorer but he has designed several bears for production.

RIGHT **"Hans-Werner Jager"** was made by the German artist **Heike Gumpp (height 52 cm/20½ in). "The Hunter"** illustrates Heike's wonderful eye for detail.

ABOVE **"Big Friendly Guy" was made by** one of the UK's best artists, **Jo Greeno** especially for the author's shop.

LEFT **"Ebenezer" was created** by New Zealanders **Michael and Judy Walton in 1993 (height 50 cm/20 in).** Artists in the southern hemisphere are beginning to receive the recognition they deserve.

ABOVE **"Gerry's Teddy at Play" was created especially for the authors by Jane Humme of the Netherlands in 1993 (height 7 cm/3½ in).**

movement grew rapidly, resulting in new and exciting teddy bears being produced at a time when collectors were really hungry for something different, individual and not too expensive. There was an immediate rapport with collectors which has grown and lasted to this day. Subsequently, the influence of the America bear artist spread to other countries and in particular to the UK, while the Netherlands, Germany, Australia, New Zealand and Japan are now beginning to develop their own artist bear markets.

American artists have given the lead which other new artists around the world should appreciate and, while still developing their own ideas, gladly follow. In the UK the standard of artist teddy bears has improved enormously to the point where the creations of some potentially excellent artists are often equal to those produced by American artists; and this is now beginning to happen in other countries too.

Without doubt the artist bear is currently the vogue, and an enormous international market has developed which is presently the most important of the three genres (old, contemporary and artists) covered in this book. This was partially because of the high prices demanded for old bears, and because contemporary alternatives were tending to become predictable and relatively far too expensive.

The tremendous variety, individuality and quality provided by artist bears probably satisfies the needs of many present day collectors, who are infinitely more sophisticated, well-informed, discerning and demanding than a decade ago.

ABOVE **This appealing bear called "Marvin" was made by Austrian artist Karin Kronsteiner in 1993 (height 70 cm/27½ in).**

BELOW **"Marvin the Magician" was made in 1993 by one of Britain's top artists – Naomi Laight. She rarely dresses her bears but Marvin shows her skilful use of antique materials.**

ABOVE **British artist Maddie Jones made "Algie" with hand-dyed mohair. He was made in 1993 and measures 45 cm/18 in.**

LEFT **There is precision and quality in Nancy Crowe's (USA) work. "Sandman" was made in 1993 and measures 38 cm/15 in.**

RIGHT **"Amelia Earheart" is one of Betsy Reum's (USA) most popular designs. She measures 25 cm/10 in and was made in 1993.**

BELOW **Rosalie Frischmann's (USA) bears are much sought after. "Murphy" was made in 1991 and measures 58 cm/23 in.**

Artists everywhere now produce store-specials, limited editions, one-of-a-kind bears, as well as charitable donations and show pieces. There is a tremendously exciting variety of bears available to collectors to suit all tastes and pockets. One of the most appealing factors, however, is that the vast majority of artists simply abhor the idea of producing large quantities of the same bear. The restricted production does of course greatly enhance future investment prospects; the one-of-a-kind bears and small quantity editions are likely to be the rarities for future generations of collectors. Of course anyone can make a single bear but it is only the special edition teddy bears produced by distinguished artists that are likely to prove the best investment prospects.

However, no one can ever be quite sure precisely what future generations of arctophiles will prefer, so why not just enjoy collecting artist bears regardless of their potential value?

ABOVE **Gregory Gyllenship** is one of a handful of British male teddy bear artists. He prefers traditional designs as can be seen from "Alexander" (seated) and "Gilbert". (Height 41 cm/16 in, 1993.)

RIGHT **Janet Clark's (UK)** captivating bear called "Sophie" was made for the Teddies of the World '93 convention. (Height 56 cm/22 in).

ABOVE **More appealing** creations from Dee Hockenberry (USA). These are called "Timeless Teddies" and measure 30 cm/12 in and 36 cm/14 in. They were made in 1993.

RIGHT "Debbie" is a teenager from the 1950s and a big Elvis fan of course! She was made by Diane Gard (USA) in 1994 in a limited edition of ten and measures 76 cm/30 in.

ABOVE Lynda Graves (UK) prefers to make very small numbers of her character bears. "Stargazer" was made in 1993 in a limited edition of three. (Height 41 cm/16 in).

ABOVE Celia Baham (USA) is a prolific and very creative artist. The "Roosevelt Bear" shown is from her second edition. He was made in 1993 and measures 46 cm/18 in.

ABOVE **Sue Quinn's popularity has spread from her native Britain to the rest of the world. "Sugar Plum Bear" was made in 1993 and measures 33 cm/13 in.**

ABOVE Billee Henderson (USA) is an award winning bear designer who can turn her hand to a range of styles. "James", a traditional bear, was made in 1993.

ABOVE These delightful clown bears named "Cornetto" and "Pauro" were made by Shirley Latimer (UK) in 1993. They measure 38 cm/15 in and 9 cm/7½ in.

ABOVE Before turning her talents to artist bears, Pam Howells (UK) was a designer for Chiltern. "Charlotte" was made in 1993 and measures 58 cm/23 in.

ABOVE American Ena Hammond creates bears with distinctive personalities. Ena made "Woolly Bear" in 1991. He measures 30 cm/12 in.

ABOVE Teresa Rowe is one of Britain's up and coming artists. The "Mad Hatter", a character from *Alice in Wonderland*, was made in 1994 and measures 30.5 cm/12 in.

ABOVE Kathy Wallace (USA) has been making bears since 1982. Her designs are traditional and full of character. "German Gold" measures 62 cm/24½ in (1991).

ABOVE Anne Inman (USA) is renowned for her innovative ideas. "Strawberries and Cream" is filled with fragranced pellets! She was made in 1993 (height 48 cm/19 in).

ABOVE **C**omposition pieces are always in demand. "The Strawberry Picker" by Linda Edwards (UK) is a stunning creation made in 1993 and measuring 43 cm/17 in.

ABOVE **These traditionally dressed bears, "Sumo bear Yokozuna" and "Kimono", were created by Japanese artist Terumi Nishiyama in 1993. (Height 13 cm/5 in.)**

LEFT **"Huxley", by Denis Shaw (USA), is an appealing interpretation of a real bear. He was made in 1993 and measures 24 cm/9½ in.**

RIGHT **"Emmett" is part of Steve Schutt's wonderful Bedy-By series. The long-limbed design is very distinctive. He was made in 1991 (height 37 cm/14½ in).**

ABOVE "Fleur" and "Ice Crystal" were made by up and coming miniaturist, Britain's Louise Peers. They were made in 1993 and measure 8 cm/3 in.

ABOVE **The quality and detail of this delightful bear by Marcia Sibol (USA) speaks for itself. "Jenny" was made in 1991 and measures 37 cm/14½ in.**

ABOVE "Mother and Baby" 6/15 cm (2⅞/6 in) by Grandma Lynn Lumley (USA) c. 1993. This Toby Award winning artist specialises in bears between 4 and 7 inches, uniquely costumed.

ABOVE **One of America's most successful artists, Janet Reeves' bears are in demand worldwide. "Miss Hildegard" was made in 1993 and measures 44.5 cm/17½ in.**

ABOVE **Mary Holden (UK) likes to keep her bears as environmentally friendly as possible by using natural wool fillings. "Baby George" measures 46 cm/18 in (1994).**

ABOVE **Michi Takahashi's (Japan) bears are always fun and these "Fairy Chuckles" are no exception. They were made in 1993 and measure 73 cm/2¾ in and 15 cm/6 in.**

LEFT **"Luke" is another example of the delightful, characterful bears being created by the talented Dutch artist Jane Humme. (Height 18 cm/7 in, 1993.)**

RIGHT **"The Applepicker" was made by Teresa Brookes and Barbara Percival (UK), who incidentally are sisters. This bear was made in 1994 and measures 33 cm/12 in.**

ABOVE **"Pearly King and Queen" were made by Nicola Perkins (UK), a top miniaturist. These two traditional British characters measure 7.5 cm/3 in.**

ABOVE **Barbara Ferrier (USA) produces bears in an enormous variety of styles. "Panda" is an unusual miniature bear made in 1991 and measuring 10 cm/4 in.**

ABOVE **"Blue Bear" is one of American Brenda Dewey's popular fantasy bears. It was made in 1993 and measures 12.5 cm/ 5 in.**

# WHERE AND HOW TO BUY

The problems facing every collector are what to collect and how much to spend. You have to decide whether collecting is purely to satisfy a love of bears, or whether it is a matter of investment. Both have quite different requirements. There are a whole host of possible sources of where to buy or sell teddy bears, all of which have advantages and, dare we say, pitfalls.

## RARITY FACTOR

However popular they all may appear, it is obvious that some teddy bears are rarer than others, usually because very few were ever made. Sometimes rarity is assumed because it may be extremely difficult to attribute a bear of undoubted quality and appeal to a specific manufacturer. Fortunately, some manufacturers are well-known and particular items can be positively identified from company records and other reliable sources; Steiff are a prime example but even with them positive substantiation is sometimes difficult. All too often reliable information about a manufacturer is scarce or even non-existent. This fact creates an awful dilemma for those with the responsibility of trying to determine authenticity.

**LEFT** *The Teddy Bear Shop* is an original painting by teddy bear lover and artist Diane Elson (1988).

ABOVE This musical bear was originally attributed to Schuco. We think it is more likely to be by Eduard Cramer.

The question of rarity is of little relevance if the particular teddy bear is so unattractive or crudely made that no one could possibly be interested. The law of supply and demand really determines the value of most bears, whether rare or not! Many contemporary manufactured limited editions become scarce after only a few years, and is not the artist "one-of-a-kind" creation potentially a rare piece?

ABOVE **A one of a kind bear that is potentially very valuable: "Old Time American** **Policeman" made by Betsy Reum (USA) in 1993 and measuring 40.5 cm/16 in.**

## PROVENANCES

As we have mentioned frequently in this book, establishing the age of a particular bear is very difficult and should never be considered a precise science – except when indisputable evidence exists, it is often a matter of judgement based on experience.

Frequently, people spurred on by the prospect that the bear may be worth a lot of money, foolishly assume that granny's bear must be about her age! A lady once tried to tell us that her bear had to be 110 years old because her grandmother (dead then, of course) had been born around 1885. She could not believe us when we said teddy bears could not be that old. She might well not have known this but didn't she realize that *nylon* teddies were not made until the 1950s! Everyone seems convinced that they know exactly their bear's age and do not like being contradicted! What is irrefutable evidence, however, is a picture of a child with a bear, preferably dated, together with other supporting written documentation.

Of course we all know of many people, often in the trade, who sadly have remarkably fertile and imaginative ideas about a bear's age and history when it comes to selling! It is always difficult to be sure any information is accurate, so be cautious.

ABOVE **This bear was sold as a 1930s Steiff teddy baby. It is in fact from the 1950s. 9 cm/3½ in** teddy babies from this era are much harder to find and so are more valuable!

ABOVE **This style of bear has often been attributed to J. K. Farnell. But this unusual white** bear from the late 1930s is unmistakably a Chiltern.

## FAKES

It is sad to reflect that with greater public awareness of the potential value of an old teddy, unscrupulous people have now taken to faking bears. If you accept that manufacturers make pretty good copies of their old bears, and that some artists are capable of producing really good old-looking bears, then you realize how easy it is to mislead the inexperienced collector. Faking can therefore be a very lucrative pastime for crooks!

Most people involved in faking bears are fairly unsophisticated, so they frequently let themselves down, though occasionally you just might come up against a good forgery, so be careful – and remember it is not necessarily the most expensive bear that can provide the forger with a good living! If you are in the slightest doubt or suspicious, leave the bear well alone!

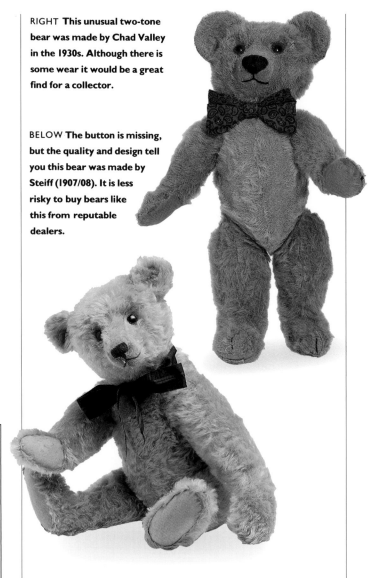

RIGHT **This unusual two-tone bear was made by Chad Valley in the 1930s. Although there is some wear it would be a great find for a collector.**

BELOW **The button is missing, but the quality and design tell you this bear was made by Steiff (1907/08). It is less risky to buy bears like this from reputable dealers.**

### HOW TO SPOT A FAKE

▌ Rub your hands fairly lightly over the bear's fur – if your hands soil easily, it is likely that the grime was recently applied.

▌ Smell the bear – it should have a natural old fusty smell and not a distinct odour of tobacco or dirt.

▌ Look at the wear and tear. Cuts and tears are rarely a precise clean cut such as one made by a knife. Mohair wear is naturally intermittent and uneven. Therefore, look closely at the backing of the pile and any fine line marks caused by wire brush or sandpaper, frequently used to enhance wear, will be obvious. A disc or brush applied to an electric drill will leave a distinct circular pattern.

▌ However well kept, most old bears of 40 or more years inevitably have suffered discoloration of some form or other. Look in the joints and you will see the bear's natural colour but expect some deterioration elsewhere. The fur of a recently made bear looks fairly consistent all over.

▌ Finally, just hold the bear because modern filled bears look and feel distinctively different from old ones, although this will require some experience to recognize.

### ATTRIBUTES TO LOOK FOR IN AN OLD BEAR

If your reason for buying is just because you love looking after old bears, then probably all you will need to do is make eye contact (with the bear, not the vendor) and if you are not immediately attracted, then you probably never will be!

First, character, which is a very subjective matter, is probably the essential factor. Condition will also be an important consideration in old bears. This is a matter of personal preference as to what you are prepared to accept. One should not expect bears to be in pristine condition; indeed well-loved bears are frequently far better characters when they have been played with.

## SPECIALIST COLLECTORS' SHOPS

In the USA, UK and the Netherlands specialist collectors' shops are plentiful and they are now beginning to spring up in other countries too. It is necessary to define what a specialist collectors' shop constitutes. In our view it is a shop that caters exclusively to the collector and not tourist or off-the-street trade, and certainly not a gift, antique or general toy shop. While many of the latter may be perfectly reliable, they cannot ever be considered in the same category as the specialist shop which has dedicated itself totally to serving collectors. Some specialist shops deal only in old bears, while others sell contemporary and artist collectibles, and some deal in all three categories.

Collectors will soon discover which shops to patronize, and those which can be entirely relied upon for their professional, ethical approach and standards. As with all collectibles, there are specialists who have been established much longer than others, are highly regarded with a reputation gained over the years for fair dealing. In general, these dealers are also capable of providing a reliable advisory service including valuation and identification.

## CHECK POINTS FOR CONDITION

Compare the colour of mohair in the joints with the rest of the bear as you can determine just how faded the bear actually is. It might be seriously faded but perhaps it has just grown old gracefully just like us humans. Mohair should generally be in satisfactory condition.

▌ The facial embroidering should match the general demeanor of the bear but if it is bright and fresh, it was probably added recently. This would not perhaps matter too much but so often the wrong style of nose or mouth is sewn, giving the bear quite a false look. Of course this could have happened 40 years before on a visit to a teddy bear hospital, which is why you need to know as much as possible about the original style of nose.

▌ Are the eyes original? There is a very good chance they they are not! If not, make sure they are the right size and colour and have been fitted properly.

▌ Are the limbs well retained or have some discreetly hidden stitches been added to anchor the head or legs?

▌ Are there any tears in the fabric, split seams, or damaged pads?

▌ Does the voice box or squeaker work? Most of them do not and sadly the modern day replacement is often poor in comparison and distinctly noticeable.

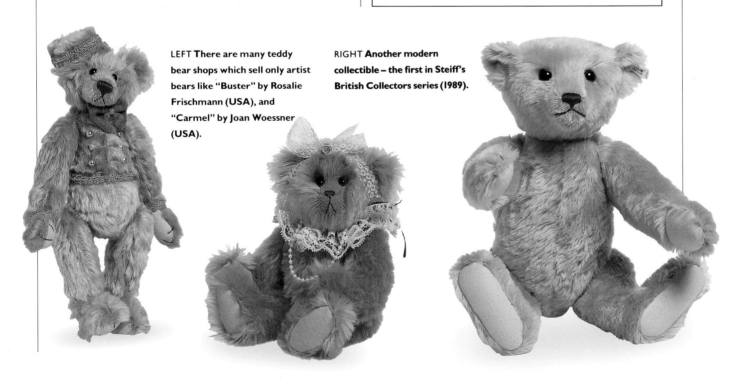

LEFT **There are many teddy bear shops which sell only artist bears like "Buster" by Rosalie Frischmann (USA), and "Carmel" by Joan Woessner (USA).**

RIGHT **Another modern collectible – the first in Steiff's British Collectors series (1989).**

## SPECIALIST COLLECTORS' FAIRS/SHOWS

Teddy bear fairs are springing up everywhere and in general the leading fairs are definitely going to be your best opportunity to seek out both old and new bears. Nowhere else will there be such quantity of delectable teddy bears because the top events usually attract the nation's best specialist shops, dealers and of course artists. At these fairs you will also meet some independent dealers who do not have shops, but many of whom will have a good selection of bears for sale. Other participants at these shows are the artists and bear-makers, providing a splendid opportunity to purchase examples of their wonderful bears directly and also learn more about their craft.

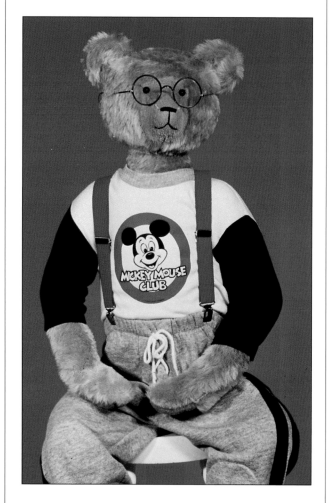

ABOVE **This is "Munchie", a one-off creation by Steve Schutt (height 90 cm/36 in). One of the great things about** **teddy bear conventions is that top artists often create special one-off bears for the auctions and competitions.**

There are now a veritable host of well-established teddy bear fairs in the USA, the UK and elsewhere. Many are well-organized and well worth attending. In addition, there is a plethora of smaller events which could well be worth visiting too; there is always the possibility that you will find something unexpected and interesting, particularly from a less experienced dealer.

## ANTIQUE FAIRS/SHOWS

At the average antique collectors' fair, you are lucky to find more than one or two dealers selling teddy bears. Usually, though not always, there are a few old bears to be found among the general dealers, but these are often poor quality, over-priced, and frequently inappropriately and ambitiously identified.

We offer a serious word of caution because, although only occasionally, it is probably at antique fairs that you are most likely to encounter a fake or even a stolen teddy bear. The gullibility of some people when confronted by a "bargain" teddy being sold by a dealer who quite clearly would sell his own granny never ceases to amaze us.

*Be warned* and *be careful*, and do not buy anything you cannot be positive about.

## TEDDY BEAR CONVENTIONS

American society was raised on conventions and it is therefore inevitable that these would be organized from the time there were enough teddy bear fanatics to attend. Although the small convention has largely given way to the likes of Disney (doll and teddy bear combined), they all remain very good opportunities for collectors, and particularly because their favourite artists or manufacturers are present to sign their bears or generally just talk.

Conventions are now beginning in other parts of the world. Teddies of the World '93 held in Northampton, UK, was exclusively concerned with teddy bears old and new and was the first of its kind with an emphasis on all facets of collecting. Japan has recently held its first collectors' convention.

At all of these events artists are usually invited to produce special one-of-a-kind bears for auction. Frequently, all the proceeds are given to charity but this is not always the case. This provides yet another excellent opportunity to obtain that really special example of an artist's work.

## AUCTION HOUSES

The UK probably has the finest auction houses in the world, all holding regular sales. Usually these are combined toy, dolls and teddy bear auctions where you can buy or arrange to sell, but you will have to pay a premium for the service of between 10 and 15%. If you want an independent assessment of potential value, auction houses are an obvious and generally accepted source.

Auction houses unquestionably have the advantage of being able to reach a much larger market because their client base includes both trade buyers and private collectors. Consequently, they are more likely to achieve prices which possibly concur with your own expectations, should you wish to sell.

ABOVE **When it comes to positively identifying your teddy bears, leading specialists are just as reliable as the** **auction houses. Left to right: 1950s Merrythought, Schuco "Yes-No" from c. 1935 and a 1920s Gebrüder Bing.**

One word of caution though – over the past few years television programmes dealing with antiques in general have shown bias in perpetuating the idea that auction houses are the only places for buying and selling. It is perfectly true they have produced some fabulously high sale prices but these are definitely the exception rather than the rule. When it comes to identification, the leading specialists are generally equal if not better.

ABOVE **It is easy to identify this Merrythought bear because of its condition and label. This is** **not always the case and specialist advice is advisable before selling.**

## ANTIQUE SHOPS

These are always worth exploring because even if you do not find any bears, you might still find some splendid teddy memorabilia or a delightful old costume for your favourite bear.

The obvious problem with antique shops is that because they have to deal with a wide range of artifacts, they generally lack specialist knowledge about bears. They also often depend on general antique pricing guides and you may well find any bears optimistically priced to put it mildly.

## CAR BOOT/GARAGE/JUMBLE SALES

We constantly get asked about the value of bears which were found at these sales. Nine hundred and ninety-nine times out of a thousand the bear is probably not of any real value but very occasionally someone has had a really good find. There is always a chance of this but, in our experience, you had better be prepared to spend many long and fruitless hours searching.

These sales can, however, be a good source for those of you who are not all concerned with the value but just want to give a new home to a poor discarded teddy. You are more likely to find teddies from the 1970s and 1980s who are in need of a more appreciative new guardian.

## MAGAZINES

Teddy bear magazines often carry "For sale" advertisements and these can be useful. However, you often have to buy sight unseen, and your interpretation

ABOVE **It is still possible to find cheap, unidentified old bears. From studying this bear, our** **guess would be that it was made by the World War I manufacturer W. H. Jones (UK).**

of pristine is likely to be quite different from the vendor's, nor can you always be sure that it is a genuine private sale. You take a chance always whether you are buying or selling.

## WHEN BUYING AND SELLING . . .

### DO

❚ Try to find out as much as you can about the bear; family photographs and other provenances are a definite advantage.

❚ Buy from reliable people.

❚ Make sure the choice is definitely yours and not a persuasive sales person's technique.

❚ Take account of the extra commission or premiums you will have to pay if buying or selling at auction.

❚ Thoroughly check the bear before purchasing to make sure it is in good condition and is what it is supposed to be. (Sometimes of course the bear has been attributed to the wrong maker which occasionally might just benefit you.)

### DON'T

❚ Do not believe everything you are told, particularly when looking at old bears!

❚ When selling, do not hand over the bear to a would-be purchaser without full payment unless they are reputable dealers.

❚ Do not buy from anyone you feel you cannot trust.

❚ Do not buy unless you are absolutely sure this is the bear you really want.

❚ Do not buy for investment only; this will prevent your being upset if the teddy bear's value does not increase as quickly as you would wish.

❚ Do not buy limited editions without their certificate or box.

❚ Do not buy inferior quality unless of course you want to. Contemporary bears which are damaged in any way should be totally avoided.

# CARE AND REPAIRS

All bears benefit from being properly looked after and the following advice may be of some guidance.

## What should I do when I bring home a newly purchased bear?

You might be surprised by what can be found inside old bears. This warm and safe habitat is a delightful haven for all types of bugs and parasites which can easily spread to the rest of your collection if you are not careful. One solution which seems to offer some protection though not total, is to wrap any newly purchased bear in a polythene bag and leave it in the freezer for at least 48 hours. As extra protection you might consider adding some flea powder (vacuum off afterwards).

Some people use moth balls but we do not advocate this method because of the smell. We discovered an old English 19th-century recipe from *Mrs Beeton's Household Management*, which advocates sprinkling whole cloves in small dishes and placing these among your bears. The smell is not strong to humans and it seems to work. Another solution is to buy impregnated wooden cedar blocks, as apparently insects do not appear to like them.

We have been asked if bears can be protected from bugs by putting them inside glass cabinets. Bugs will usually get in despite this but it will of course help to keep the bears clean.

Remember, you constantly need to inspect your teddies and clean them.

LEFT Jo Greeno's "Miss Marple" and Gary Nett's (USA) "Father Christmas" investigate the mysterious death of a 1905 centre seam Steiff!

RIGHT With a little care and attention this Steiff bear from the 1920s can be brought back to pristine condition.

### How should I clean my bears?

Mohair, alpaca and wool are the main materials used for making old bears and being natural fibres, these are all washable. However, never immerse a teddy in water – it would have a devastating effect – wash the surface of your bears only.

Use a mild detergent mixed with warm water and whisked to produce a foam (test first that this does not make the material fade). Using a soft cloth or a soft baby's brush, rub or stipple this into the mohair. Do not use a stiff or hard bristle or nylon brush as this may damage the backing of the fabric or pull out the fibres. Stubborn stains can be removed by the use of a bristle toothbrush (soft to medium), but be careful.

When you are satisfied (you can soon tell as your bowl of water should be discoloured), remove the suds with a clean wet cloth. After the suds have been removed, go over the bear again with warm water to which a little fabric conditioner has been added, and rub this all over the bear. Afterwards rub the surface carefully with a clean towel to remove excess moisture.

A hairdryer set to low heat is a very useful way of quick drying but remember how you dry your own hair, and using the same technique (no rollers please!), continually brush the fabric if you wish to "style" or control the lay of the pile. When the bear is dry, we always place it in the airing cupboard for 48 hours because this will dry out the bear slowly and thoroughly.

It is often very difficult to clean a teddy bear made of synthetic materials, although you can try the same method as given above. However, these bears were often manufactured to enable them to be totally immersed in water so you may therefore be able to wash them by hand (check the label). Remember teddy would not like to take a trip in your washing machine or tumble dryer!

### How should I regularly clean my bears other than by surface wash?

Inspect your bears regularly for infestation, dust and so on, and keep the fur clean by vacuuming them. Be careful that you do not apply excessive suction – it will be all too easy to skin a bear or remove a loose eye or that valuable name tag or label. Guard against this by covering the vacuum nozzle with a nylon stocking.

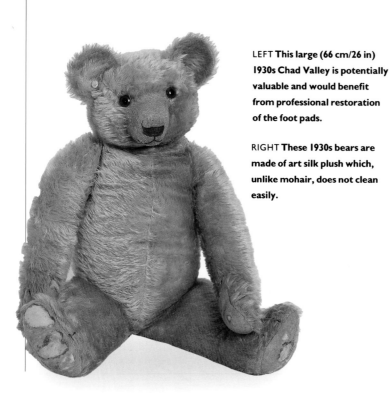

LEFT **This large (66 cm/26 in) 1930s Chad Valley is potentially valuable and would benefit from professional restoration of the foot pads.**

RIGHT **These 1930s bears are made of art silk plush which, unlike mohair, does not clean easily.**

**If I really cannot bring myself to subject my teddy to surgery, what other practical hints can you advise?**

Damaged hand and foot pads can be temporarily protected by using babies' gloves and booties. Frail bodies, arms and legs can also be well protected by dressing teddy in an old one-piece babygrow, or simple cardigan and trousers.

**Do bears and live animals go well together?**

No because it is well-known that dogs and cats can carry all sorts of fleas and other bugs, which might just be looking for a new habitat! Also no teddy would enjoy being picked up and shaken in a dog's mouth, or clawed by a cat, any more than you would.

**Will smoking have any effect on my bears?**

Bears are affected by passive smoking just as humans are because the smell lingers in their fur – but it's really up to you. We do not allow anyone to smoke in our shop or in our home, and that way our teddies smell fragrant.

**I am worried about insuring my collection what should I do?**

You should definitely get your bears catalogued and properly insured. This is not as expensive as you might think and even though much of your collection might be irreplacable, at least adequate insurance will be some recompense should something happen. We recommend that you also get an effective security alarm system installed, including fire detection, as this will almost certainly be in your favour when applying for insurance and, of course, give you peace of mind.

Make a careful list with as much information as possible about your bears – date of purchase, how much they cost, size, make and so on. It may also be necessary to obtain an independent valuation by a teddy bear specialist but this probably depends on how valuable your collection is and how comprehensive your records are. Photographing all your bears is another good idea but it is so much easier, quicker and cheaper to video them. Remember to make duplicate copies and deposit them in the bank or some other safe place, but not in your house in case it was ever seriously damaged.

LEFT **It is probably too late to do much more than a careful surface wash on this 1938 Merrythought Dutch boy.**

RIGHT **This 1930 Chad Valley has also suffered the ravages of time and it is best just to give it a surface wash.**

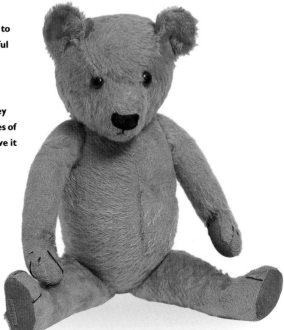

### What if my bear needs repairing?

If your bear is in need of major repair or restoration or if it is very valuable, then we would recommend the services of a reputable bear repairer or hospital. Check the credentials of the repairers first and ask to see some of their work, or better still ask to speak to someone who has used the repairer before. We would *never* advocate your attempting major repair yourself unless you are experienced!

If your bear needs a minor repair, you may feel competent enough to tackle this yourself. A split seam or loose pad can easily be repaired, provided you are competent with a needle and thread. Should you need to re-darn a nose, mouth or paw, make sure you use the came colour floss. *Never* change the pattern of these features – always copy exactly the method of application used by the manufacturer. This is not as easy as it looks and you can totally destroy the character of your bear.

Eyes should only be replaced if one is broken or missing. Here again you must try and match the original eye both in colour and size. To ensure teddy has the right eyes, pads or facial features, thorough research in this and the many other authoritative books that exist. Remember many old bears have had their noses and eyes changed, so if the opportunity arises, make sure you replace them by the correct style or type of eye. Most eyes are sewn to the lower back of the head but some were sewn through the ears. If in doubt get the work carried out by a proper repairer.

### Why has my teddy discoloured over the past few years if he has only been kept in the living room?

No fabric, except some manmade fibres, tolerates direct exposure to sunlight. *Always keep bears away from direct or excessive sunlight.* In fact keep the curtains closed as much as possible to reduce the amount of light in the room. Lace curtains will also help to cut down light penetration. Move your teddies around the room constantly so that none of them get more sunlight than is good for them. Unlike humans, a teddy bear will not get a tan if left in the sun, but more likely a most unhealthy pale complexion (due to discoloration)!

LEFT **This 1960s Chiltern Hugmee looks much better after a wash and brush up.**

RIGHT **A 1930s Merrythought that has been partially bleached by strong light.**

# LEARNING
# MORE ABOUT
# BEARS

In order to derive the maximum benefit from collecting teddy bears, you owe it to yourself, and your Bank Manager, to obtain as much knowledge as is possible. The more proficient you are at identifying old bears, recognizing a good bargain, or appreciating investment potential (this applies to both new and old bears), the less likely you are to make a serious – and therefore costly – mistake. The following sources may help to improve your knowledge.

## MUSEUMS

Although there are a great many toy museums, we frequently find those which claim to have "many teddy bears" rarely do and are thus rather disappointing. This is particularly true of those in Germany. We would, however, suggest that whenever possible, you should try to make a visit because even if a museum contains only a few examples, these can all enhance your appreciation of teddy bears. These are just a few museums you should *not* miss:

**USA**
The Teddy Bear Museum of Naples, Florida

**UK**
The Cotswold Teddy Bear Museum, High Street, Broadway, Worcestershire WR12 7AJ
The Bear Museum, 38 Dragon Street, Petersfield, Hampshire GU31 4JJ

**GERMANY**
Margarete Steiff Museum, Allen Strasse 2, D-7928 Giengen (Brenz)

RIGHT **Examine your bears thoroughly – this 1930s Chad Valley had a button attached to the back of the shoulder adding to its value.**

LEFT **Gary Nett's (USA) "Mr Cinammon" bear is in a studious mood. He was made in 1983 and measures 41 cm/ 18 in.**

## SHOWS AND CONVENTIONS

These can be both tremendous fun and beneficial in providing opportunities to add to your collection and share joyful experiences with other collectors. There are a considerable number of events in the U.S. and Europe, but only the very best shows and conventions attract the big names in the teddy bear world.

### U.S.A.

ABC Unlimited Promotions Shows, Schaumberg, Illinois, and other locations (several)

Bill Boyd's Teddy Bear Jubilee, Kansas City, Missouri (annual)

Serena Cohen's, Libearty Weekend Artist Bear Show, Philadelphia, Pennsylvania (annual)

Disneyland Doll and Bear Convention, Anaheim, California (annual)

Disney World Doll and Bear Conventions, Florida (annual)

Donna Harrison's Shows and Convention, Baltimore, Maryland (twice yearly)

ILTBC Convention, Orange, California (annual)

Linda Mullins Shows, San Diego, California (twice yearly)

Steve Schutt's Teddy Bear Reunion in the Heartland, Clarion, Iowa (every five years, next in June 1995)

### JAPAN

Japan Teddy Bear Association Convention, Tokyo (annual)

### BRITAIN

Margaret and Gerry Grey's Teddies of the World Convention, location to be confirmed (every three years, next in 1996)

Hugglets, Teddy Bear Fairs, and events, London and Stratford-on-Avon (several)

Teddy Bear Times, British Bear Festivals, Croydon, and Hove, East Sussex (twice yearly)

### THE NETHERLANDS

Rob and Inge Kuiters, Bear Festival Amerongen Castle (every May)

## MAGAZINES

There are many very good specialist magazines published throughout the world which you will find an extremely valuable source of information.

Bear Facts Review, published in Australia

Beer Bericht, published in the Netherlands (four issues)

Ciesliks Teddy und seine Freunde, published in Germany

de Teddy-Beer, published in the Netherlands (four issues)

Hugglets Teddy Bear Magazine, published in U.K. (four issues)

Teddy Bear and Friends, published in U.S.A. (six issues)

Teddy Bear Review, published in U.S.A. (five issues)

Teddy Bear Times, published in U.K. (six issues)

## RECOMMENDED READING

There are many wonderful books, all of which we unfortunately cannot list here. Every single teddy bear book you can lay your hands on should be read, because with each one there is always something new to learn and improve your knowledge. Particular books we would positively recommend as very useful and entertaining are the following:

Peter Bull, Teddy Bear Book (1969)

Jurgen and Marianne Cieslik, Button in the Ear (1989)

Hobby House Teddy Bear & Friends Price Guides – Nos. 1, 2, 3, and 4 (1993)

Pauline Cockrill, The Ultimate Teddy Bear Book (1991), and The Teddy Bear Encyclopedia (1993)

Dee Hockenberry, Collectible German Animals Value Guide 1948 to 1968 (1989), and Bear Memorabilia (1992)

Margaret Hutchings, The Book of the Teddy Bear (1964)

Ted Menten, Teddy's Bearzaar (1988), and Teddy Bear Lovers Companion (1989)

Linda Mullins, Teddy Bears Past and Present, Vol I (1986) and Vol II (1991)

Romy Roeder, Teddy Bears, Golliwogs and Playmates of the Past (1988)

Patricia N. Schoonmaker, A Collector's History of the Teddy Bear (1981)

Rosemary and Paul Volpp, A Beary Merry Christmas (1987), and A Bear for all Seasons (1989)

Carol-Lynn Rössell Waugh, Teddy Bear Artists – Romance of Making and Collecting Bears (1984)

## CLUBS AND ASSOCIATIONS

These are obviously worth considering because you will be able to meet people with similar interests. There are now a vast number of collectors' clubs; some associated with manufacturers such as the Steiff Club, some with magazines such as the Teddy Bear Times British Bear Club, the International League of Teddy Bear Clubs in the U.S., and those with solely charitable intentions such as Good Bears of the World – covering just about every conceivable facet of collecting.

Our personal preference is, however, for the less formal type of small local self-run clubs such as the one we belong to called the Bear Talk Club, in Stratford-on-Avon, England.

Details of clubs and associations are listed regularly in leading collectors' magazines.

# INDEX

**A**

Acton Toy Craft Ltd 34
Aerolite 20, *20*, 22
Aetna 13
  "Still Hope" *11*
Ahsolight 20
American Doll and Toy
  Manufacturing Co 14
antique shops and fairs 70, 71
Applause 41
Atlas Manufacturing Co 15
auctions 71
Australian bears
  inter-war 28–9
  post-war 37–9
Austrian bears 39

**B**

Baham, Celia
  "Roosevelt Bear" *62*
Baxter, Thomas 16
Beacock, Brian "Buster" 58
Bearly There Inc 41
Berg 39
Berg, Herman 10
Berlex Toy Pty 28, 37, *37*
Berryman, Clifford 9, 10
Bing, Gebrüder (later Bing-
  Werke) 12, *12*, 17, 26, *26*
Bingie bear 24, *24*
Blackburn, John and Maude 41
  "Rosie" *41*
books, teddy bear 78
Borgfeldt, Geo 10, 14
Boston, Wendy
  Playsafe bears 32, *32*
British United Toy
  Manufacturing Co 16
Brookes, Teresa and Percival,
  Barbara
  "The Applepicker" *65*
Bruin Manufacturing 13
Bull, Peter 6, 8, 42, 55
Butler Bros 14
buying bears 66–72

**C**

Calvin, Karin and Howard 57
Canham, Deborah
  circus bears *54*
Canterbury Bears 41, *41*, 42
Chad Valley
  Aerolite 20, *20*, 22
  dating 22
  inter-war bears 7, 20, *20*,
    21–3, *22*
  Magna 22
  Peacock 22, *22*, 23
  post-war bears 30, *30*, 32, *32*
Character Novelty Co 31, *31*
Chiltern bears
  Baby Bruin 34
  Cubby 25
  early bears 15–16
  Hugmee 24, *25*, 34, *34*, 76
  inter-war 20, 24–5
  Master Teddy 1915 *15*
  post-war 34

Silky Teddy 20
Skater Bear *25*
Ting-a-Ling Bear 34
Clark, Janet
  "Loving" *55*
  "Sophie" *61*
  cleaning bears 73–5
clubs and associations 78
Columbia Teddy Bear
  Manufacturing 14
  Laughing Roosevelt Bear *14*
Commonwealth Toy and Novelty
  Co
  "Feed me" bear 21
condition of bears 68–9
Conley, Barbara *8*
  "Antique Gray Bear" *57*
conventions 70
Cramer, Eduard 28
Cranshaw, Anne 57
  "Casco Bear" *57*
Cray and Nicholls 16
Crowe, Nancy
  "Sandman" *60*

**D**

dating bears 22, 67
Deans Rag Book Co Ltd
  collectibles 42
  earliest bears 15
  inter-war 23, *23*
  post-war 33, *33*
Dehler, E. 18
Dewey, Brenda
  "Wizard" 54, "Blue Bear" *65*
Dreamland Doll Company 14

**E**

East London Toy Factory
  (EALON) 16, 25
Edwards, Linda
  "The Strawberry Picker" *64*
Eisemann, Josef 16
ELI 18
Emil Toys 28, *29*, 38, *38*
Epstein, B. 14

**F**

FADAP 29
fairs, specialist 70
fakes 68
Farnell, J. K.
  Alpha 23
  early bears 12, 15
  inter-war 7, *19*, 20, 23, *23*
  post-war 33, *33*
  Silkalite 20
Fast Black Shirt Co 14
Ferrier, Barbara
  "Panda" *65*
French bears 29
Frischmann, Rosalie
  "Buster" *69*
  "Murphy" *60*

**G**

Gard, Diane
  "Billy Ray" 55, 57
  "Marisa Bearensen" *56*

"Debbie" *61*
German bears
  early manufacturing 9,
    10–11, 12, 17–18
  inter-war years 19, 21, 26–8
  limited editions 43–53
  post-war 35–37
Gillespie, Mrs G. C. 14
Gottschalk and Davis 16
Graves, Lynda
  "Stargazer" *62*
Greeno, Jo
  "Miss Marple" *54*, 73
  "Big Friendly Guy" *58*
Gumpp, Heike
  "Hans Werner Jager" 58
Gund Manufacturing Co 14, 21,
  31
Gyllenship, Gregory
  "Alexander" and "Gilbert" *61*

**H**

Hammond, Ena
  "Woolly Bear" *63*
Harman Manufacturing Co 13
Harmus, Carl, Jr 18
Harwin and Company 15
  Ally Bears 15
Hecla Bear Co 13
Helvetic 29
Henderson, Billee
  "James" *62*
Hercules bears 17
Hermann, Gebrüder
  early bears 12, 18
  inter-war 28
  post-war 35, *35*
  replicas 43, *43*
  Zotty 35
Hermann, Max (later Hermann-
  Spielwaren) 18, 27, 37
Hockenberry, Dee
  "Mr Bruin" *57*
  "Timeless Teddies" *61*
Hofmann, Carl 18
Holden, Mary
  "Baby George" *65*
Horsmann, E. C. and Co 14
Howells, Pam
  "Charlotte" *63*
Hughes, Herbert E. 16
Humme, Jane
  "Gerry's Teddy at Play" *59*
  "Luke" *65*
"Humpty Dumpty" toys 17
Hutchings, Margaret 55

**I**

Ideal Toy and Novelty Co 10, 13,
  *13*, 31
  "Charlamagne" *10*
Imperial Toy Co 16
Inman, Anne
  "Strawberries and Cream" *63*
insects, protection from 73
Institute of Hygiene mark of
  approval 20
insurance 75
Invicta Toys 25

Isaacs (ISA) 16, 22
Isenberg, Barbara 41

**J**

Jakas 38
Japanese bears 19, 30, *64*, *65*
Jones, Maddie
  "Algie" *60*
Jones, W. H. 17
Joy Toys Pty 29, *29*, 38, *38*
Jumbo Toys 17

**K**

Knickerbocker Toy Co Inc 19,
  21, *21*, 31, *31*
Kronsteiner, Karin
  "Marvin" *59*

**L**

Laight, Naomi
  "Marvin the Magician" *59*
Lakeland Bears 42
Latimer, Shirley
  "Cornetto" and "Pauro" *62*
Leco Toys 34
Lefray Ltd 34, *35*
Leven, H. Josef, and Sprenger
  18, 28
Liebermann, Ernst, and Co 18
light, protecting from 76
Lindee Toys 39, *39*
Lines Brothers/International
  Model Aircraft Co Ltd *see*
  Pedigree
Little Folk 42
Lumley, Grandma Lynn
  "Mother and Baby" *64*

**M**

Madingland 17
magazines, 78
  buying from 72
Magna bears 22
Magnet bear 24
MAHESO 18, 28
Menten, Ted 56
  "Hug" 41, *41*
Merrythought Ltd 19, 24, 33
  Bingie 24, *24*
  Cheeky 33, *33*
  limited editions 42
  Magnet 24
  Punkinhead 33
Michtom, Morris and Rose 9–10
MICHU 18
Millas Manufacturing Co 14
Mutzi N. C. Z. 39

**N**

Nett, Gary and Margaret
  "Father Christmas" *54*
  "Mr Cinnamon" *77*
Nisbet, House of 42–3
  Bully Bear range 42
  Celebrity Collection 43, *43*
  Delicatessan 42, *42*
  Zodiac range 42
Nishiyama, Terumi
  "Sumo Bear Yokozuma" and
  "Kimono" *64*

North American Bear Co 41
  Hug 41, *41*
  Muffy 41
  V.I.P. range 41
  Vanderbear 41

**O**

Oppenheimer, S., Ltd 35

**P**

Peacock bears 22, *22*, 23
Pedigree 25, *25*, 33
Peers, Louise
  "Fleur" and "Ice Crystal" *64*
Perkins, Nicola
  "Pearly King and Queen" *65*
Petz Co 37
Pintel, M., Fils and Cie 29
Playsafe bears 32, *32*
Plummer and Wandless and Co
  Ltd 35
Port, Beverley 56

**Q**

Quinn, Sue
  "Sugar Plum Bear" *62*

**R**

Raikes, Robert, Originals 41
rarity 66–7
Rees, Leon, and Co *see* Chiltern
  Bears
Reeves, Janet
  "Miss Hildegard" *65*
repairing bears 76
replicas and special editions
  40–53
Reum, Betsy
  "Amelia Earheart" *60*
  "Old Time American
    Policeman" *67*

"Puppeteer" *58*
Riley, Kathryn
  "Bearlin the White Wizard"
    55
Roosevelt, Theodore 9
Ross Toy Works 17
Rössel-Waugh, Carol-Lynn 56
  "Jenny-Lynn" *56*
Rouech-Bowden 14
Rowe, Teresa
  "Mad Hatter" *63*

**S**

Schuco (Schreyer and Co) 12,
  26, 36
  Bellhop bear 26
  Piccolo range 26, *26*
  Tricky 36
  tumbling bears 26
  Yes-No bear *20*, 21, 26, 35
Schutt, Steve 57
  "Emmett" *64*
  "Munchie" *70*
Shaw, Denis 57
  "Huxley" *64*
  "Ursus" *57*
shops, specialist 69
shows and conventions 78
Sibol, Marcia
  "Jenny" *64*
  "Lady Margaret" *64*
silk plush bears, introduction of
  20
soft filled bears, introduction of
  10
"Softanlite" bears 17, 20
South Wales Toy Manufacturing
  Co 17
Steevans Musical Toys 17
Steiff, Margarete
  Barle range 10–11

British Collection series *40*,
  *52*, 69
button trademark 7, 11
"Christian Gabriel" *10*
Circus bears 27, 46
"Dicky" *27*, 46
"Edelweiss" 7
earliest bears 7, 10–11, *12*,
  18, *18*
European Collectors Club 53
"Happy" 21, 44
"Jackie" 37, 48
"King Arthur" *16*
"Margaret Strong" 44, *44*
inter-war *20*, 27, *27*
limited editions 40, *40*,
  44–53
model 5322 11
PAB range 11, 18, *18*
Petsy range 27, *27*, 50
post-war *36*, 37, *37*
"Richard Steiff" *46*
"Teddy Clown" 27, *46*
"Teddy Rose" *48*
USA Collectors Club 53
Zotty 7, *36*, 37
Steiff, Richard 9, 21
Stone, H. G. and Co Ltd *see*
  Chiltern
Stuffed Toy Co bears *12*
Süssenguth, Gebrüder
  Peter bear *20*, 28, *28*
Swiss bears 29, *39*

**T**

Tah Toys Ltd 25
Takahashi, Michi "Fairy
  Chuckles" *65*
Teddy Toy Company 17, 20, 25
  Softanlite 17, 20, 25

Terry, W. J. (Terryer Toys) 16,
  20
Thiennot 29
Tinka-Bell 35
Twyford bears 34

**U**

UK bears
  early distributors 16–17
  early manufacture 12, 15–16
  inter-war years 19, 21–5
  limited editions 41–3
  post-war years 32–5
  teddy bear artists 59
US bears
  early distributors 14
  early manufacture 9–10,
    11–12, 13–14
  inter-war years 19, 21
  limited editions 41
  post-war years 30, 31
  teddy bear artists 55–9
Uncle Remus Stuffed Toys 14

**V**

Verna 39, *39*
Very Important Bear (V.I.B.)
  range 41

**W**

W. T. Co 35
Wallace, Kathy
  "German Gold" *63*
Walton, Michael and Judy
  "Ebenezer" *58*
Whiteson Company 14
Wholesale Toy Company 17
Wilson, Jack 42

# ACKNOWLEDGMENTS

(Key: l = left, r = right, m = middle, be = below, t = top)

It would be impossible to write a book of this type without the assistance of others. We should particularly like to thank:

Des and Monica Carpenter, and son Mark, of The Cotswold Teddy Bear Museum, who allowed us to disrupt their splendid displays in order to photograph the lovely bears. (Bears on pages 7tl & bm, 15, 17br, 20tr & bl, 21, 22 bl & br, 23tl, tr & br, 24tl, tr & bl, 25bl, 26br, 33bl & br, 34bl, 35tl & tr, 66r, 68t, 71, 72, 73r, 74, 75l, 76, 77r.)

Sue Pearson, 13 Prince Albert Street, The Lanes, Brighton, East Sussex BN1 1HE, UK, who can always offer the finest old bears. Sue allowed us to raid her shop one day and take her treasured bears away to be photographed in a nearby studio. (Bears on pages 11l, 12m, 13r, 17tr, 18, 20bm & br, 23bl, 26tr, 27bl & br, 30, 33t, 67br, 68b.)

Romy Roeder, who kindly provided us with photographs of some of her own Australian bears. (Bears on pages 29, 37r, 38, 39.)

Paul and Rosemary Volpp, who generously allowed us to use some specially selected examples from their superb Buck Hill Teddy Bear Collection. (Bears on pages 6r, 7br, 10, 11ltr & r, 12l & r, 13l, 14, 16, 27t, 31.)

All the artists who allowed us to illustrate this book with wonderful examples of their imaginative and creative teddy bears. Unfortunately it was not possible to include every bear that was photographed – our apologies to these bears and their owners. Thank you to the artists who lent their own bears. They appear on the following pages: 54br, 55m, 56tl, 61br, 57tm, 58tm, tr & br, 59tr & br, 60tl & tr, 61tl & tr, 62tl, tr & br, 63tl & 64tl & 65mr & bl, 70.

Bears on 53l courtesy of Margarete Steiff GmbH, 67bl courtesy of Anne Greaves and 54tl from a private collection. All other bears are owned by the authors and are either part of their private collection or can be found at their shop at 7 Cambridge Street, Wellingborough, Northants, UK NN8 1DJ.

Very special thanks to Quintet Publishing and the photographers, Nick Bailey and Jeremy Thomas, for all their patience.

And lastly a special thank you to daughter, Jenny, who managed to sort out our scribbles and type the manuscript.